# PAM AYRES
## The Works

# PAM AYRES
## The Works

### THE CLASSIC COLLECTION

*With illustrations by Susan Hellard*

BBC BOOKS

First published in 1992 by BBC Books
This revised edition first published in 2008
Published in paperback 2010
BBC Books is a Random House Group company.

9 10 8

The Random House Group Limited Reg. No. 954009
Addresses for companies within the Random House Group can be found at
www.randomhouse.co.uk

A CIP catalogue record for this book is available from the British Library.

ISBN 9781846077937

Commissioning editor: Christopher Tinker
Designer: Linda Blakemore
Copy-editor: Helen Armitage
Production: David Brimble

Printed and bound by CPI Group (UK) Ltd, Croydon, CR0 4YY

The Random House Group Limited supports The Forest Stewardship Council
(FSC®), the leading international forest certification organisation. Our books
carrying the FSC label are printed on FSC® certified paper. FSC is the only forest
certification scheme endorsed by the leading environmental organisations, including
Greenpeace. Our paper procurement policy can be found at
www.randomhouse.co.uk/environment

# Contents

# *Introduction*

to the 1992 edition

In this book I would like to offer you a selection of the noble works. Some of these date from about 1974 when I was writing pieces like 'The Battery Hen' and 'Oh, I Wish I'd Looked After Me Teeth'. At that time I was working for a company which bought bits to go inside car heaters. As you can imagine, this was a fascinating and deeply fulfilling job, shot through with suspense and excitement. I worked in a long, thin office where people tended to walk sideways. Through the window you could thrill to the view of two gasometers ponderously rising and falling during the course of the day. Writing the poems came as a welcome relief.

I started performing those poems and a few ill-chosen songs ('Johnny I Hardly Knew Ye', 'My Soldier Boy Wears a Blue Cockade') at our local folk club at The Bell Inn in the village of Ducklington. I remember the disbelief I felt when I was offered £12 to do a guest spot at a pub called The Railwayman's Arms up near Nether Heyford. I only had to do half an hour and at the time I was earning £20 *a week*! I recall driving up there, white with terror, my guitar on the back seat. Years later I played famous places like the London Palladium and the Sydney Opera House, but I was never quite so nervous as on that night at The Railwayman's Arms.

Well, then I was befriended by BBC Radio Oxford. Folk music was more popular then, and Radio Oxford used to send people around recording choice bits at local clubs for their weekly programme. They must have come to The Bell on a good night when I was not singing 'My Soldier Boy Wears a Blue Cockade' because they decided that some of my pieces were choice and that started a very happy relationship during which I had a weekly spot on the radio. I always say to people who write verse and are looking for a market that the local radio is worth a try. BBC Radio Oxford were very helpful to me.

The first time I sat in front of a TV camera was in 1975 at Thames Television. The programme was a talent show called *Opportunity Knocks* and I was sandwiched between a man who sang 'You Are My Heart's Delight' and a woman who played the squeeze box. It was a very terrifying experience, especially as the bus bringing my family had got lost on the way and I desperately wanted them in the audience. The bus in question was emblazoned with the legend 'Crapper's Coaches' down the side so it was easy to spot. Anyway, all was well and I won. I seemed to get a lot of work after that, though I felt poorly qualified for it. It was one thing to proclaim to a cider-mellowed group of mates in Ducklington Folk Club, and another to be thrust out in front of two thousand people who had paid good money in some vast hall in Wolverhampton. My main recollection is of being absolutely terrified of the next job.

At about that time I wrote two pieces I was especially pleased with. They were 'Thoughts of a Late-Night Knitter' and 'The Ballad of Bill Spinks' Bedstead'. I've never been at all interested in writing topical things, you know, something pointed about the politicians of the day. It takes just as long to do but has a very short life indeed. I was always pleased with 'Oh, I Wish I'd Looked After Me Teeth' as a choice of subject and I think it is likely to tickle people for as long as we chew sweets and fear the dentist's drill.

In fact I like writing about people most of all. I think there is a huge amount of humour in our small human failings and in the way we try to justify our actions and hang on to our dignity. I love the great disparity between the way a man might see himself compared with the way others see him.

After I got married and had our two sons, I felt as if the real world had opened up. I think children are a great leveller and I can see now how squeamish I was before. I was preoccupied with what to wear and what I looked like. Preciously, I claimed that I couldn't watch young children eating because the way they ended up with food all round their faces turned my delicate stomach. However, pregnancy, birth, sleepless nights, three month colic and a baby given to robust milky burps punctured all this pompous twaddle. My mother said, 'We all have to come to it' and I came to it.

What I also came to, by marrying and having children, was a new world to write about. Family life has always seemed to me to be a rich picking-ground. 'Once I Was a Looker and So Was My Spouse' came from this time, and 'Don't Start!' about the way we talk to our children. I think there is more real humour to be found in family life than in any elaborately constructed gag.

More recently I've been writing about our gallant attempts to fight off ageing, as in 'Do You Think Bruce Springsteen Would Fancy Me?' People ask me if I'm afraid of running out of ideas but I'm not, no, because I've always written as a sort of commentary on what I see, almost like a diary. I can't imagine losing that inclination, having had it for so long.

Sometimes people ask me if I'm from a theatrical family. My uncle Les used to 'play the mouth organ beautiful' so I'm told, and my brother Allan did have a brief dalliance with a trumpet at the time when Eddie Calvert's gut-wrenching 'Oh My Papa' was all the rage. Unfortunately, the early morning practice sessions were too much for our own papa, who emerged from his bedroom one morning, his eyes white with the light of battle, and wrested the instrument from his grip. Allan gave up the trumpet from a sense of self-preservation. So I think, on reflection, that I'm not from a theatrical family, no.

People ask me if I think of myself as a poet and the answer is no, I don't. I call them poems because it's simple, it trips off the tongue, Pam's poems. It's cleaner than Pam's rhymes or Pam's comic verses. Poetry seems to be a very serious and profound business, and I was essentially looking for something to make people laugh.

I hope you enjoy this book. I never actually wrote these pieces to be read in silence, but always to be proclaimed out loud, with gusto. I hope if you have any favourites that they are included and I hope they make you laugh, in which case I will be extremely happy.

*Pam Ayres* 1992

# Introduction

This is the first time that *The Works* has been available in a hard-back edition, and I am very pleased to see it looking so smart and substantial.

These are my first poems, the ones I started writing for fun in the sixties, then more conscientiously from the seventies, when I realised with mounting excitement and disbelief that people were prepared to spend money to see me perform them. I wrote them from the time I was a young woman concerned with my various pets and boyfriends, through marrying and bringing up a young family, to the start of the downward spiral: the looking in the mirror, those first grey hairs, the crow's-feet, the gammy knee.

When I approached this new edition, I fully intended to drop some of the old poems because looking at them now, decades after they were first written, some appear so amateurish and, well, *early*. The peculiar thing is, though, that for every old one I was going to discard, someone has stopped me in the street at one time or another and said it was *that very one* that was their all-time favourite, the piece that had made them titter for years. So I have now come to the conclusion that perhaps I shouldn't start pruning at this late stage, and that they should all be left in, so that anyone who is interested can see where I started, the kind of thing I was writing and performing from my early twenties.

For me the poems fall into two categories. At first I wrote them as a joke, just a means of raising a laugh, because I enjoyed it so much and thought anybody who felt so inclined could do the same. It's fairly easy to spot those. Gradually, though, I began to see a change. People offered to *employ* me to perform my poems, and it slowly dawned on me that perhaps my ability wasn't so commonplace after all. It might even prove to be an enjoyable way to earn a living, doing something that I truly loved, tinkering about endlessly with words to produce something funny that would make people laugh. All my previous jobs had been of a clerical sort, concerned with matters in which I had no interest, where I sat and typed and watched the clock along with everyone else.

Once the joyful possibility had opened up, I stopped thinking of the poems as a joke and tried to produce the very best work I could. This is the second category, where I started to apply myself seriously to the task. My objective was always straightforward: to write something with which the audience would identify, which, if I performed it well, would make them laugh and send them home feeling better.

I am delighted to say that some of these poems, like 'Pam Ayres and the Embarrassing Experience with the Parrot', 'Oh, I Wish I'd Looked After Me Teeth', 'The Battery Hen' and 'In Defence of Hedgehogs', have reached an even wider audience than I had ever envisaged and are included in school textbooks throughout the world. I am still regularly asked to perform them today, and 'The Battery Hen' seems even more topical now than when I wrote it.

I hope you enjoy this new edition. I have added introductions to many of the poems, and Susan Hellard has contributed her brilliant illustrations. Happy reading!

*Pam Ayres* 2008

# The Works

# The Dolly on the Dustcart

In 1975 I appeared on a television talent show called *Opportunity Knocks*, which I won. As a result, every aspect of my life changed, and I gave up my secretarial job on Friday 13 February 1976 to see if I could make a living on my own.

A rather thin book was published, and I was sent off on a promotional tour that involved me being taken at high speed to any newspaper office, radio or television station prepared to talk to me. Once there I would be offloaded, ushered in, interviewed and encouraged to declaim in verse.

At first it was cracking. I felt very important, and for the first time in my life stayed in good hotels – any previous trips away from home having been to a caravan at the seaside. However, the process seemed never-ending. For weeks and months I trailed round the UK, and I felt two strong feelings. The first was intense, grateful excitement that people were buying my book; the second was increasing homesickness. The posh hotels started to pale, and I missed my home and family. I missed being able to choose what I did with my own time.

One day I was being taken at high speed to a radio station in Glasgow. I had never been there before, and the road ran alongside the River Clyde, which was grey and swollen in the January light. I felt very lonely and homesick, and did not much fancy reciting 'Oh, I Wish I'd Looked After Me Teeth' yet again.

At some point another vehicle caught my eye. Travelling towards us on the opposite side of the road came the municipal dustcart. Affixed to the radiator grille, in a kind of crucified position, was a child's dolly. There she dangled as some sort of mascot pinioned to the metal, looking filthy, dishevelled and woefully out of place. As the dolly and I passed each other we exchanged a glance. This is what the dolly said.


### The Dolly on the Dustcart

I'm the dolly on the dustcart,
I can see you're not impressed,
I'm fixed above the driver's cab,
With wire across me chest,
The dustman see, he noticed me,
Going in the grinder,
And he fixed me on the lorry,
I dunno if that was kinder.

This used to be a lovely dress,
In pink and pretty shades,
But it's torn now, being on the cart,
And black as the ace of spades,
There's dirt all round me face,
And all across me rosy cheeks,
Well, I've had me head thrown back,
But we ain't had no rain for weeks.

I used to be a 'Mama' doll,
Tipped forward, I'd say, 'Mum'
But the rain got in me squeaker,
And now I been struck dumb,
I had two lovely blue eyes,
But out in the wind and weather,
One's sunk back in me head like,
And one's gone altogether.

I'm not a soft, flesh coloured dolly,
Modern children like so much,
I'm one of those hard old dollies,
What are very cold to touch,
Modern dolly's underwear,
Leaves me a bit nonplussed,
I haven't got a bra,
But then I haven't got a bust!

But I was happy in that doll's house,
I was happy as a Queen,
I never knew that Tiny Tears,
Was coming on the scene,
I heard of dolls with hair that grew,

And I was quite enthralled,
Until I realised *my* head
Was hard and pink ... and bald.

So I travel with the rubbish,
Out of fashion, out of style,
Out of me environment,
For mile after mile,
No longer prized ... dustbinised!
Unfeminine, Untidy,
I'm the dolly on the dustcart,
And there's no collection Friday.

## In Defence of Hedgehogs

This was one of my very first efforts. I wrote it in 1972 or 3, when I worked for a company in Witney while living at home in Stanford-in-the-Vale. Every morning I drove to work in my Morris 1000, which I hated because it did not match my aspirations in life. It clearly demonstrated how hard up I was, emitted vast, noxious clouds of smoke from the exhaust and dismally failed to present the driver as a stylish class act. Indeed, people doubled up laughing as I passed.

My route to work took me past a wood called Hatford Warren, where on most mornings at that early hour a fresh crop of squashed hedgehogs would lie flattened on the road, having been run over the night before. I found this inestimably sad, hedgehogs being charming, harmless little creatures with endearing black noses and helpful traits like the scoffing of slugs in the garden.

## *In Defence of Hedgehogs*

I am very fond of hedgehogs
Which makes me want to say
That I am struck with wonder
How there's any left today.
For each morning as I travel,
And no short distance that,
All I see are hedgehogs,
Squashed. And dead. And flat.

Now, hedgehogs are not clever,
No, hedgehogs are quite dim
And when he sees your headlamps,
Well, it don't occur to him
That the very wisest thing to do
Is up and run away.
No! he curls up in a stupid ball
And no doubt starts to pray.

Well, motor cars do travel
At a most alarming rate,
And by the time you sees him,
It is very much too late.
And thus he gets a-squasho'd,
Unrecorded but for me,
With me pen and paper,
Sittin' in a tree.

It is statistically proven,
In chapter and in verse,
That in a car-and-hedgehog fight,
The hedgehog comes off worse.
When whistlin' down your prop shaft,
And bouncin' off your diff,
His coat of nice brown prickles
Is not effect-iff.

A hedgehog cannot make you laugh,
Whistle, dance or sing,
And he ain't much to look at,
And he don't make anything,
And in amongst his prickles,
There's fleas and bugs and that,
But there ain't no need to leave him,
Squashed. And dead. And flat.

Oh, spare a thought for hedgehogs,
Spare a thought for me,
Spare a thought for hedgehogs,
As you drink your cup of tea,
Spare a thought for hedgehogs,
Hoverin' on the brinkt,
Spare a thought for hedgehogs,
Lest they become extinct.

## Thoughts of a Late-Night Knitter

I knitted furiously all through my teens. Mum taught me how to do it when I was very small, and I can still remember the chant of 'Needle in, wool round, slip it off' repeated interminably as she was demonstrating. It was a good skill to have, though, and as I got older it was a welcome means of providing myself with cheap new clothes. All the girls I knew did it, and we carried our knitting paraphernalia in conker-brown gondola baskets from Wantage market.

We bought our wool from the wool shop in Wantage, but a cheaper system was to send to the woollen mills for their samples. These came on long cards sprouting multi-coloured strands of wool, ranging from the dirt cheap and string-like to more costly and luxuriant yarns, all priced at so much an ounce. Armed with whatever wool I could afford at the time, I produced innumerable jerseys and cardigans, some a lot more successful than others. Always mad keen to get my hands on the finished item, I tended to sacrifice care for speed so that my garments suffered from the 'up at the back, down at the front' syndrome. I would constantly have to correct the look by giving a good yank down at the back.

Fashions came and went. Wool with coloured flecks, mohair, chunky knits, designs with dropped shoulders, raglan sleeves, shawl collars, I clicketty-clacked my way through them all and sported the resulting modes round Stanford-in-the-Vale.

The idea for this poem came to me years later in the more sumptuous setting of the London Palladium on the day I was appearing in *The Silver Jubilee Royal Variety Show*. It was a whole day of hanging about while the vast cast rehearsed and practised their acts with the musicians. I had 12 minutes on my own in the show, with no music, so I was soon processed and left to my own devices for the day. I found myself in a deserted red-plush bar with the grilles down. I had this idea of telling a story interspersed with an unlikely commentary on something mundane and unrelated. At first I was going to use a kind of Native American dancing-round-the-campfire chant and tell my story against that, but then I thought of a person relating a tale while knitting and working slowly or fast, as tragedy or indignation dictated. I liked this idea for two reasons: firstly, it used my vast and detailed knowledge of knitting and, secondly, I found it satisfyingly daft.

## Thoughts of a Late-Night Knitter

I had a lovely boyfriend,
Knit one, purl one.
Had him for a long time,
Cast on for the back.
Had him all the summer,
Loved him, cuddled him,
Push it up the knitting pin
And gather up the slack.

Well he *knew* how much I liked him,
Knit one, purl one.
I made him seven jerseys,
Never did him any wrong,
And he told me that he loved me,
Knit one, purl one.
Told me that he loved me
But he didn't stop for long.

Well he never said he'd left me,
Knit one, purl one.
He never even told me
No, I found out on me own.

I was going up the chip shop,
Knit one, purl one.
And he walked out the pictures
With that horrid Mary Stone.

Well I didn't know what hit me,
Knit one, slip one.
After I'd looked after him
It wasn't very nice,
And they went off down the High Street,
Laughin', gigglin',
And left me on the corner
With me chips as cold as ice.

Well it isn't that I miss him,
Knit one, drop one.
I never even think of him
Good riddance ... ta ta!
I'm very independent!
Snap one, tie one.
I've never been so cheerful,
Ha ha ... ha!

And I hear they're getting married,
Knit one, drop nine.
I wish them every happiness,
It's *lovely* staying in!
Well I don't need romancing,
Cuddlin', dancin'.
Bundle up the knitting bag
And fling it in the bin.

## Oh, I Wish I'd Looked After Me Teeth

Before leaving to work for myself, I was employed for six years as a shorthand typist by a company called Smith's Industries in Witney, Oxfordshire, and my last position was as secretary to a gentleman called Ernie. Smith's was an engineering company, producing clocks, watches, hydraulic lifting equipment, ventilation systems and navigational aids, and I had not the slightest interest in any of it.

I was bored and sullen, and Ernie did his best to enthuse me by rhapsodising about previous secretaries who'd worked for him.

'Do you remember June?' he used to ask. 'My former secretary? No, I expect she was a little bit before your time. But my goodness, what a Tartar she was! What a Tartar! She'd be in here, in my office, every Monday morning polishing my desk! Yes, she'd have all my papers arranged in neat piles –'

I used to think, 'Dream on, mush!'

I should have moved on, really, but I was nervous about leaving. As far as I could see, other available jobs were just more of the same anyway: being a secretary in some environment in which you had no interest. At that stage I couldn't have hoped to make a living from my own writing. But I went on doing it, during evenings, weekends and, it has to be said, at work when I was supposed to be typing. I wrote my own stuff and concealed it down the side of the typewriter where nobody else could see.

One day I had to go to the dentist. I had his last appointment at six o'clock in the evening, which meant that I had all day to worry about it. I wrote this piece at Smith's to console myself and to make light of a situation that frightened me.

## *Oh, I Wish I'd Looked After Me Teeth*

Oh, I wish I'd looked after me teeth,
And spotted the perils beneath
All the toffees I chewed,
And the sweet sticky food.
Oh, I wish I'd looked after me teeth.

I wish I'd been that much more willin'
When I had more tooth there than fillin'
To give up gobstoppers,
From respect to me choppers,
And to buy something else with me shillin'.

When I think of the lollies I licked
And the liquorice allsorts I picked,
Sherbet dabs, big and little,
All that hard peanut brittle,
My conscience gets horribly pricked.

My mother, she told me no end,
'If you got a tooth, you got a friend.'
I was young then, and careless,
My toothbrush was hairless,
I never had much time to spend.

Oh I showed them the toothpaste all right,
I flashed it about late at night,
But up-and-down brushin'
And pokin' and fussin'
Didn't seem worth the time – I could bite!

If I'd known I was paving the way
To cavities, caps and decay,
The murder of fillin's,
Injections and drillin's,
I'd have thrown all me sherbet away.

So I lie in the old dentist's chair,
And I gaze up his nose in despair,
And his drill it do whine
In these molars of mine.
'Two amalgam,' he'll say, 'for in there.'

How I laughed at my mother's false teeth,
As they foamed in the waters beneath.
But now comes the reckonin'
It's *me* they are beckonin'
Oh, I *wish* I'd looked after me teeth.

## The Battery Hen

Along with 'Oh, I Wish I'd Looked After Me Teeth', this is prob-
ably one of my best-known early poems, and for the life of me I
can't remember exactly why I wrote it. Our family kept chickens –
for eggs, of course, and because my mother abhorred waste. I think
all families who went through the hardship of World War II felt the
same. You wasted nothing. Every scrap of left-over food was fed to
the chickens. Every vegetable peeling, apple core and rock-hard disc
of ancient suet pudding was whacked over into the chickens' run
and thereby went to help produce eggs. They were the fag-end of
our recycling operation, long before recycling was ever heard of.

I was used to seeing hens out in the sunshine, scratching about and investigating as they do. When I learnt that other luckless birds were stacked in cages in airless sheds for their short, wretched lives, I found it unbearably sad. Now I don't buy laying hens from commercial suppliers, I re-home battery hens. I've got ten at the moment, and I find it good for the soul. They arrive bald and scraggy, gawping in amazement at the sunshine and grass. Soon they are feathered up, portly and hanging round the back door, getting under people's feet. It's lovely to see. I get fresh eggs, ravaged borders and the satisfaction of having enhanced the quality of a few small lives.

## The Battery Hen

Oh, I am a battery hen,
On me back there's not a germ,
I never scratched a farmyard,
And I never pecked a worm.
I never had the sunshine
To warm me feathers through.
Eggs I lay. Every day.
For the likes of you.

When you has them scrambled,
Piled up on your plate,
It's me what you should thank for that.
I never lays them late,
I always lays them reg'lar,
I always lays them right,
I never lays them brown,
I always lays them white.

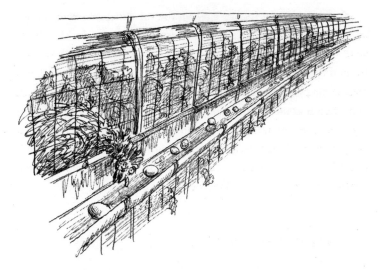

But it's no life for a battery hen.
In me box I'm sat,
A funnel stuck out from the side,
Me pellets comes down that.
I gets a squirt of water,
Every half a day,
Watchin' with me beady eye,
Me eggs roll away.

I lays them in a funnel,
Strategically placed
So that I don't kick 'em
And let them go to waste.
They rolls off down the tubing
And up the gangway quick,
Sometimes I gets to thinkin',
'That could have been a chick!'

I might have been a farmyard hen,
Scratchin' in the sun,
There might have been a crowd of chicks,
After me to run.
There might have been a cockerel fine
To pay us his respects,
Instead of sittin' here,
Till someone comes and wrings our necks.

I see the Time and Motion clock
Is sayin' nearly noon.
I 'spect me squirt of water
Will come flyin' at me soon,
And then me spray of pellets
Will nearly break my leg,
And I'll bite the wire nettin'
And lay one more bloody egg.

## The Bunny Poem

I am a bunny rabbit
Sitting in me hutch.
I like to sit up this end,
I don't care for that end much.
I'm glad tomorrow's Thursday,
'Cause with a bit of luck,
As far as I remember
That's the day they pass the buck.

## The Wasp He Is a Nasty One

The wasp he is a nasty one
He scavenges and thrives,
Unlike the honest honey bee
He doesn't care for hives.
He builds his waxy nest
Then brings his mates from near and far
To sneak into your house
When you have left the door ajar.

Then sniffing round for jam he goes
In every pot and packet,
Buzzing round the kitchen
In his black and yellow jacket.
If with a rolled-up paper
He should spot you creeping near
He'll do a backward somersault
And sting you on the ear!

You never know with wasps,
You can't relax, not for a minute.
Whatever you pick up – Look out!
A wasp might still be in it.
You never even know
If there's a wasp against your chest,
For wasps are very fond
Of getting folded in your vest.

And he *always* comes in summer.
In the wintertime he's gone
When you never go on picnics
And you've put a jersey on.
What other single comment
Causes panic and despair
Like someone saying, 'Keep still!
There's a wasp caught in your hair!'

But in a speeding car
He finds his favourite abode.
He likes poor Dad to swat like mad
And veer across the road.
He likes to watch Dad's face
As all the kids begin to shout,
'Dad! I don't like wasps!
Oh where's he gone, Dad? Get him *out*!'

And I'd like to make a reference
To all the men who say,
'Don't antagonise it
And the wasp will go away,'
For I've done a little survey
To see if it will or won't,
And they sting you if you hit them
And they sting you if you don't.

As we step into the sunshine
Through the summers and the springs,
Carrying our cardigans
And nursing all our stings,

I often wonder, reaching for the blue bag
Just once more,
If all things have a purpose
What on earth can *wasps* be for?


## The Flit Gun

My mother had a Flit Gun,
It was not devoid of charm,
A bit of Flit,
Shot out of it,
The rest shot up her arm.


## How I Loved You, Ethel Preedy, with Your Neck So Long and Slender

How I loved you, Ethel Preedy,
With your neck so long and slender.
At the Tennis Dance
What magic charm did you engender!
Our eyes met in the crowd,
Your fingers tightened on the racquet,
But when I tore my gaze away
Some swine had pinched me jacket.

## *I Am a Drystone Waller*

I am a Drystone Waller.
All day I Drystone Wall.
Of all appalling callings,
Drystone Walling's
Worst of all.

# Little Nigel Gnasher

I know all about biting your nails. I bit mine from the age of six and have found it almost impossible to control. Over the years I have coated them with every horrible product on the market and enviously watched women in the check-out queue as they probed their purses with exquisite pink, almond-shaped nails.

I would have liked healthy, wholesome-looking ones. I never craved long blood-red talons, a French manicure where they laboriously whiten the underside of the tip, or a 'full set' of those thick acrylic jobs that glitter on top while your natural nails gasp below. Just ordinary nice nails.

I don't know why I bite them – it would be handy to have some gut-wrenching trauma in my infancy to blame, but I can't think of one. Bitten nails look so ghastly. I once sat opposite a cracking-looking young woman on a train during a long journey, and she chewed her fingernails throughout. It was awful to see: the nibbling, the angling of the head, the constant working at it hour after hour. I'd like to say, 'I never did it again after that,' but I did.

I had a shock, recently, on finding a friendly website called How Can I Stop Biting My Nails? There was a photograph intended to galvanise and mortify. The caption read 'Fingernails of an Extreme Nail Biter', but they were better than mine! I was bolstered by reading the supportive comments and tips of so many other nibblers, though, and have finally managed to grow a decent set. I don't know how long I'll be able to keep them, but they feel lovely. I gesture languidly with my hands all the time and look affected. This website might even have helped poor, beleaguered Nigel Gnasher but, alas, the internet was a bit before his time.

## Little Nigel Gnasher

Little Nigel Gnasher was his name,
He bit his nails.
When other boys were having fights
Or finding slugs and snails,
You always knew that Nigel
Would be at his normal station,
Beside the rails he bit his nails
Eyes shut for concentration.

His mother tried to stop him
But young Nigel's ears were shut.
She wrapped his hands in woolly gloves,
But Nigel Gnasher cut
Straight through the flimsy fabric
With his sharp and practised teeth
And bit the helpless fingernails
That sheltered underneath.

Mrs Gnasher took him
To the Doctor one fine day.
The Doctor looked at Nigel's nails
And quickly looked away,
Saying, 'Calcium deficiency
Has laid these nails to waste.'
And he gave the lad a bag of chalk
But he didn't like the taste.

Oh he bit them on the landing
And he bit them on the stair.
Nigel Gnasher bit his nails
Till there was nothing there.
Nigel Gnasher bit them
Till he couldn't stand the pain
And then he'd summon up his courage
And bite them all again.

When other people rested
Hands outstretched on the settee,
Nigel sat upon his hands
So people wouldn't see.
He plastered them with Dettol,
Savlon, Germolene and more,
He'd have it done by half past one
And bite it off by four.

One day a local millionaire
Was driving round about.
He spotted Nigel Gnasher
And impulsively leaned out
Crying, 'Here's a present, sonny,

From eccentric Jeffrey Krupp,'
And a fiver hit the ground,
But Nigel *couldn't pick it up*!

And then the local bully,
Carver Clay, he came along
And though his head was short,
His fingernails were very long.
He pushed aside poor Nigel
Who lay clawing at the ground
And ran off with the fiver
Shouting, 'Look what I have found!'

So the moral of this story,
Little Gnashers far and wide,
Is, don't bite them up the middle
And don't bite them down the side,
Don't bite them front or sideways,
Spare your poor nails from the habit,
Then if someone throws a fiver
They will be on hand to grab it!

## Oh No, I Got a Cold

I am sitting on the sofa
By the fire and staying in,
Me head is free of comfort
And me nose is free of skin.
Me friends have run for cover,
They have left me pale and sick
With me pockets full of tissues
And me nostrils full of Vick.

That bloke in the telly adverts,
He's supposed to have a cold.
He has a swig of whatnot
And he drops off, good as gold,

His face like snowing harvest
Slips into sweet repose.
Well, I bet this tortured breathing
Never whistled down his nose.

I burnt me bit of dinner
'Cause I've lost me sense of smell,
But then, I couldn't taste it,
So that worked out very well.
I'd buy some, down the café
But I know that at the till
A voice from work will softly say,
'I thought that you were ill.'

So I'm wrapped up in a blanket
With me feet upon a stool,
I've watched the telly programmes
And the kids come home from school.
But what I haven't watched for
Is any sympathy,
'Cause all you ever get is:
'Oh no, keep away from me!'

Medicinal discovery,
It moves in mighty leaps,
It leapt straight past the common cold
And gave it us for keeps.
I'm not a fussy woman,
There's no malice in me eye,
But I wish that they could cure
the common cold. That's all. Goodbye.

## *The Curlers Poem*

A set of heated rollers
Is every maid's delight.
It stops you wearing curlers
In the middle of the night.
It keeps you looking spick and span,
When all the rest are not,
And though your hands are freezing cold,
Your head is nice and hot.

## I'm a Starling ... me Darling

Our mother was a very kind person who encouraged us from an early age to respect and care for all animals, and in particular to feed the birds. My Uncle Sam worked on the railways and made us a bird-table out of railway sleepers. It was sturdy. If a pterodactyl had flapped down and perched upon it, it would not have flinched.

We put out the usual stuff. We hung up half a coconut, threaded peanuts on to strings, tied up little bundles of bacon rind, crumbled up bits of bread and cake, knobs of dripping, anything we thought they might like. Then we would rush indoors and wait behind the curtain to see what came. We hoped to see the beautiful native birds – the blackbird with his golden beak, a marvellous speckled thrush, dear little blue tits, shy wrens with their sticking-up tails, pink chaffinches and a vibrant red-breasted robin. Arrive they did, too, in a wondrous parade, as we watched stock-still and holding our breath behind the curtain. It was magical but short-lived.

Soon one starling would arrive and swagger round the banquet. Then another. To groans from the spectators the sky turned black. A vast multitude of starlings would descend on the food like a plague of locusts and scoff the lot. Our bird-table was picked clean. The bird-watching was over, and it was time to find something else to do.

Nobody liked starlings then. There were just so many of them, and they seemed so greedy. None of us thought for a moment that those enormous flocks filling the evening sky would diminish in the way they have.

I quite like starlings now.

## I'm a Starling ... me Darling

We're starlings, the missis, meself and the boys.
We don't go round hoppin', we walks,
We don't go in for this singing all day
And twittering about, we just squawks.

We don't go in for these fashionable clothes
Like old Missel Thrush, and his spots,
Me breast isn't red, there's no crest on me head,
We've got sort of, hardwearing ... dots.

We starlings, the missis, meself and the boys,
We'll eat anything that's about,
Well, anything but that old half coconut,
I can't hold it still. I falls out.

What we'd rather do is wait here for you
To put out some bread for the tits,
And then when we're certain you're there by the curtain,
We flocks down and tears it to bits.

But we starlings, the missis, meself and the boys,
We reckon that we're being got at.
You think for two minutes, them finches and linnets,
You never sees them being shot at.

So the next time you comes out to sprinkle the
    crumbs out,
And there's starlings there, making a noise,
Don't you be so quick to heave half a brick,
It's the missis, meself and the boys!

## *The Hegg*

A thrush, disconsolate, with no sign of a mate,
Sat morbidly perched in a tree,
Saying, 'I tell the tale
Of a flighty young male,
Who have done the dirty on me.

'I'm Hexpecting a Hegg, a Hillicit Hegg,
A Hegg lyeth here, in my breast.
While the trees were bright-leaved
I rashly conceived
A Hegg, Houtside of the Nest.

'For my deed I am shunned, and left moribund,
And by all I am left on a limb.
I would give my right wing,
To be rid of this thing,
And for my great girth to be slim.'

Just then a black crow, with his black eyes a-glow,
Boldly down to the thrush flew,
Said, 'The grapevine, I've heard,
Tells of a distressed bird,
Which I've reason to think may be you.'

He stood on one leg, said, 'You're having an Egg
And the other birds feel you are bad.
But if with me you came,
You'd be free of the shame,
Of having an Egg with no dad.

'For a nominal fee, I will take you to see
My friend, who lives up the back doubles.
If you swear not to fail
To pay on the nail,
He will duff up the source of your troubles!'

So the thrush, unafraid, assented and paid,
And went under cover of night
To see an old Bustard,
With gin and with mustard,
And to be relieved of her plight.

She was made to sit in a bathful of gin,
And she was obliging and meek.

She was made to consume
Some soap and a prune,
And her feathers fell out for a week.

Outside on the bough, she said, 'Look at me now,
Of my Hegg I am freed, but I'm Hill,
And if Hagain I stray
Without naming the day
Then first I shall go on the Pill.'


## Puddings – a Slice of Nostalgia

Don't open no more tins of Irish Stew, Alice,
You know it makes me pace the bedroom floor,
You gave me Irish Stew a week last Sunday,
And I never got to sleep till half past four,
You open up another tin of spam, Alice,
Or them frankfurter sausages in brine,
And we'll stab them, sitting opposite each other,
And you can dream your dreams, and I'll dream mine.

I'll dream about me apple cheeked old mother,
Her smiling face above a pot of broth,
She used to cook us every sort of pudding,
Proper puddings ... in a pudding cloth!
When we came home from school all cold and hungry,
One look along the clothes line was enough,
And if the pudding cloth was there a-flapping,
We all knew what it meant – a suet duff!

A suet duff would set your cheeks a-glowing,
Suet duff and custard, in a mound,
And even if you'd run about all morning,
A suet duff would stick you to the ground,
Or else there'd be a lovely batter pudding,
With all the edges burnt so hard and black,
That if your teeth had grown a bit too long like,
Well, that would be the stuff to grind them back.

She used to make us lovely apple puddings,
She'd boil them all the morning on the stove,
If you bit on something hard that wasn't apple,
The chances were, you'd bitten on a clove,
Or else there'd be a great jam roly poly,
We'd watch it going underneath the knife,
And if you took a bite a bit too early,
The red hot jam would scar your mouth for life.

Oh bring back the roly poly pudding,
Bread and butter pudding ... Spotted Dick!
Great big jugs filled up with yellow custard,
That's the sort of pudding I would pick,
But here's the tube of artificial cream, Alice,
I've cleaned the nozzle out, the hole's so fine,
And we'll squirt it on our little pots of yoghurt,
And you can dream your dreams, and I'll dream mine.

## Like You Would

This was one of my very early efforts inspired, if that is the word, by a friend I liked very much. He and I went out a few times – a trip to the cinema, a pleasant drink in the sunshine. However, he had an irritating mannerism. Regardless of what you said to him, he would begin his reply by saying, 'This is the thing, you see …' It never varied, and it drove me nuts. I found I was steeling myself, waiting for him to say it. He probably didn't realise how automatic it had become. You could say, 'My, what a pleasant spring day it is!' or 'I have contracted bubonic plague in both legs' and back would come the mindless retort, 'Well, this is the thing you see …' Now I would make some light-hearted joke about it, try to make him realise he was doing it and wean him away from it, but then I didn't have the confidence; it didn't seem appropriate for me to try to correct another person. The romance stumbled and foundered.

Like it would.

### *Like You Would*

Well, I got up in the morning,
Like you would.
And I cooked a bit of breakfast,
Like you would.
But at the door I stopped,
For a message had been dropped,
And I picked it up, and read it,
Like you would.

'Oh, Blimey!' I said,
Like you would.
'Have a read of this,
This is good!'
It said: 'I live across the way,
And admire you every day,
And my heart, it breaks without you.'
Well, it would.

It said: 'I'd buy you furs and jewels,
If I could.'
And I go along with that,
I think he should.
It said: 'Meet me in the park,
When it's good and dark,
And so me wife won't see,
I'll wear a hood.'

Oh, I blushed with shame and horror,
Like you would.
That a man would ask me that,
As if I could!
So I wrote him back a letter,
Saying, 'No, I think it's better
If I meet you in the Rose and Crown,
Like we did last Thursday.'


## Love Is Like a Curry

Love is like a curry and I'll explain to you,
That love comes in three temperatures, cold, hot
     and vindaloo.
Of course it's like a curry, it cannot be denied,
For both are full of spice and both have dishes on
     the side.


## I Am a Witney Blanket

I am a Witney Blanket,
Original and Best.
You'll never get cold feet
With me across your chest.

## *Oh Don't Sell Our Edgar No More Violins*

Oh don't sell our Edgar no more violins,
That dear little laddie of mine,
Though he's but eight, we'd prefer him to wait,
Or I doubt if he'll live to be nine.
He plays the same song, and it's sad, and it's long,
And when Edgar reaches the end,
With his face full of woe, he just rosins the bow,
And starts it all over again.

Now Daddy says Edgar's a right little gem,
It's only Daddy's *face* that looks bored,
It's really delight makes his face appear white
When Edgar scrapes out that first chord.
Daddy of course, he was filled with remorse,
When Edgar came home from the choir,
To find that his fiddle, well, the sides and the middle,
Were stuffed down the back of the fire.

So don't sell our Edgar no more violins
When next he appears in your shop,
His daddy and me, we are forced to agree,
His fiddlin' will soon have to stop.
Sell him a clean, or a filthy magazine,
Ply him with whisky or gin,
A teddy! A bunny! or just pinch the kid's money,
But don't sell our Edgar no more violins.

For though it be a mortal sin,
We'll do the little fiddler in,
Don't sell our Edgar no more violins.

# I Don't Want to Go to School, Mum

My sister Jean had children long before I did and produced two beautiful daughters. They were soon toddling about and talking, but I had not reckoned on how obstructive little girls can be when someone, clearly an impostor, turns up wishing to talk to their mum, distracting her from her rightful duties. It was no longer possible to have an uninterrupted conversation with my sister by day, and by the evening she was as shattered as all mums. I had always had free access to her and, selfishly, I missed our easy, friendly chats.

Eerily, one of the girls acquired an imaginary friend called Boy. When I sat down on the sofa I would receive precise instructions to sit forward, sit back, move up, etc., so that Boy could see the TV. I obliged, of course, but it was very strange because to any other person in the room there was no Boy to be seen on the sofa at all.

This piece came from those random childish interruptions.

## *I Don't Want to Go to School, Mum*

I don't want to go to school, Mum
I want to stay at home with my duck.
I'd rather stay at home with you, Mum,
And hit the skirting board with my truck.
Don't make me go to school today, Mum,
I'll sit here quiet on the stairs
Or I'll sit underneath the table
Scratching all the varnish off the chairs.

I don't want to go to school, Mum
When I could be underneath your feet.

It's shopping day and we could go together
Taking twice as long to get to Regent Street.
And every time you stop to talk to someone
I won't let you concentrate, no fear,
I'll be jumping up and down beside you
Shouting 'Can I have some sweets, Mum?' in your ear.

Or how about me doing a bit of painting?
Or what about a bit of cutting out?
Or sitting in the open bedroom window
Body in and legs sticking out?
Or what about us going up the park, Mum?
Or how about me sitting at the sink?
Or what about me making you a cake, Mum?
And Mum. Hey, Mum. Mum, can I have a drink?

Mum, what's that at the bottom of the cupboard?
And Mum, what's in that bag you put down there?
And hey, Mum, watch me jump straight off the sofa,
And Mum, whose dog is that stood over there?
What you doing, Mum? Peeling potatoes?
Sit me on the drainer watching you
I wouldn't *mind* me trousers getting wet, Mum.
Oh I aren't half fed up. What can I do?

What time is Daddy coming home, Mum?
What's in that long packet? Sausage meat?
How long is it before he comes, Mum?
And Mum. Hey, Mum. What can I have to eat?
Oh sorry, Mum! I've upset me Ribena.
Oh look! It's making quite a little pool.
Hey, Mum, hey, where we going in such a hurry?
Oh, Mum! No, Mum, you're taking me to SCHOOL!

## Goodbye Worn Out Morris 1000

Oh love, you got no poke left
I didn't want to say,
It seems we are outmoded,
Much too slow, and in the way,
You know how much I love you;
I'd repair you in a flash
But I haven't got the knowledge
And I haven't got the cash.

There is rust all round your headlamps,
I could push through if I tried.
My pot of paint can't cure it
'Cause it's from the other side.

Along your sides and middle
You are turning rusty brown,
Though you took me ninety thousand miles
And never let me down.

Not the snapping of a fan belt
Nor the blowing of a tyre
Nor the rattling of a tappet
And nor did you misfire.
All your wheels stayed on the corners
And your wipers on the screen
Though I didn't do much for you
And I never kept you clean.

All your seats are un-upholstered
And foam rubber specks the floor.
You were hit by something else once
And I cannot shut the door.
But it's not those things that grieve me
Or the money that I spent,
For you were my First-driven,
Ninety thousand miles we went.

I could buy a bright and new car
And go tearing round the town
A BGT! A Morgan!
(With the hood all battened down).
But as I leave you in the scrapyard,
Bangers piled up to the skies,
Why do your rusty headlamps
Look like sad, reproachful eyes?

## *Goodwill to Men: Give Us Your Money*

It was Christmas Eve on a Friday,
The shops was full of cheer,
With tinsel in the windows,
And presents twice as dear.
A thousand Father Christmases
Sat in their little huts,
And folk was buying crackers
And folk was buying nuts.

All up and down the country,
Before the light was snuffed,
Turkeys they got murdered,
And cockerels they got stuffed.
Christmas cakes got marzipanned,
And puddin's they got steamed,
Mothers they got desperate,
And tired kiddies screamed.

Hundredweights of Christmas cards
Went flying through the post,
With first-class postage stamps on those
You had to flatter most.
Within a million kitchens,
Mince pies was being made,
On everybody's radio,
'White Christmas', it was played.

Out in the frozen countryside,
Men crept round on their own,
Hacking off the holly
What other folks had grown.
Mistletoe from willow trees
Was by a man wrenched clear,
So he could kiss his neighbour's wife
He'd fancied all the year.

And out upon the hillside
Where the Christmas trees had stood,
All was completely barren
But for little stumps of wood.
The little trees that flourished
All the year were there no more,
But in a million houses
Dropped their needles on the floor.

And out of every cranny, cupboard,
Hiding place and nook,
Little bikes and kiddies' trikes
Were secretively took.
Yards of wrapping paper
Was rustled round about,
And bikes were wheeled to bedrooms
With the pedals sticking out.

Rolled up in Christmas paper,
The Action Men were tensed,
All ready for the morning,
When their fighting life commenced.

With tommy guns and daggers,
All clustered round about,
'Peace on Earth – Goodwill to Men',
The figures seemed to shout.

The church was standing empty,
The pub was standing packed,
There came a yell, 'Noel, Noel!'
And glasses they got cracked.
From up above the fireplace,
Christmas cards began to fall,
And trodden on the floor, said:
'Merry Xmas, to you all.'

## The Swimming Song

I like to swim
I'll meet you after school
It keeps us trim
I'll see you down the pool
It keeps us fit
Watch out we're on the prowl
We do our bit
Talcum powder and a towel
Both great and small
Watch us on the diving board
Life savers all
Duke of Edinburgh's Award
If we're around
We're demons in the drink
You won't get drowned
We never ever sink.

We swim like fish
Cod, kipper, cockle, carp
Here, there, gone, swish!
Oh play it on your harp
And diving too
In the deep dark dregs
Just me and you
We'll be laughing at the legs
Just name the stroke
Oh, the butterfly and crawl
And I'm your bloke

Will you give me back my ball?
I love to spring
Plunge plink plonk paddle
It makes me sing
Tra la diddle daddle.

We're in the shower
Shampoo soap scrub
For half an hour
Rub a dub a dub a dub
Do you know that
Dad gave me fifty pence
You aren't half fat
Ouch! Eek! No offence!
It's great to swim
Never any pain or ache
It keeps us slim
Would you like a piece of cake?
So after school
If you have an hour to spend
Come to the pool
We'll race you to the end.

## *Plughole Serenade*

Would you care to come sailing with me love,
For the wind couldn't puff out a candle.
We'll drag the tin bath up the old garden path
And you have the end with the handle.

*I wrote this for a 'dump old drugs' campaign, to discourage people from hoarding ancient medicines.*

### Dump It!

Have you, in your cupboards dusty, medicines grown
    old and fusty,
kept for some forgotten pain, in case it should come
    back again?
Or tablets very kindly lent, by whatisname wherever
    he went,
which cured his sinus like a charm, but never touched
    your broken arm?

Take the packages so neat, the courses you did not complete,
any job that's now been jobbed, for anything that ached
    or throbbed,
soothing jars of ancient unction, meant for bits that
    ceased to function,
any joint that loudly creaked, or any part of you that
    leaked.

Oh dump it, dump it, dump it all, far away from
    fingers small,
and older folk who get confused. Take any drug that's
    partly used,
any ointment, pills or potion, linctus, liniment or lotion,
resolutely in your fist and *dump* it on your pharmacist.

For drugs and poisons it is true, are safer far with him
    than you.

# Ever Since I Had Me Op

My mum gave me a lot of good advice, though I didn't value it much at the time. One small but weighty nugget was this: never get Too Thick with your neighbours.

I moved into a terraced house, and one of my neighbours was an elderly lady whom I am sure was lonely. She was nice; I liked her and at first we used to chat over the garden fence. Once having started this amiable trend, though, I soon realised that not only was she a person who had unfortunately undergone many surgical operations but also someone more than happy to tell you about them. Indeed, it was exceedingly difficult to get away. Once having uttered the reckless words 'How are you?' the floodgates opened, and you would find out. The date and minute details of each operation would be listed, the exclamations of each astonished surgeon, culminating in almost every case with a lurid and ghastly description of the thing I came to dread: the growth as big as a grapefruit. Hours would elapse before I could eventually break away and get back indoors. I longed for fresh air and sunshine but did not dare go into my garden. I stopped buying grapefruit. I had fallen into the trap, failed to heed my mother's advice and got Too Thick with my neighbours.

## *Ever Since I Had Me Op*

Hello, it's nice to see you looking well,
What? How am I?
I haven't been so good myself
But I've been getting by

No, I've had a bit of trouble
Well, I wouldn't bore a friend
But if you knew how much I'd suffered
Well, your hair would stand on end.

No, I'm not one to complain
And we all have our cross to bear
And I wouldn't even tell you
What they did to me in there
If you asked how many stitches
I wouldn't let it cross me lips
Well alright then, twenty-seven
And that's not including clips.

Course, it was only fifty-fifty
On the drip all night and day
Oh they gave me all the lot
And then they took it all away
You wouldn't have recognised me
And I'm glad I never seen ya
And the doctor on the case
Gave up and went back home. To Kenya.

Well, I know you're in a hurry
And you haven't time to stop
And I've just seen Deirdre
She'll want to know about me op
And there's always someone worse off
Than yourself, without a doubt,
In my case I haven't met him
But I'm sure that he's about.

And you're healthy dear, enjoy it
For it fades away so soon,
Now I've got me eighteen pills
So I'll get through this afternoon
Don't give a thought to how I've suffered
I'm the last one to complain
I'll just keep smiling through it all
Until we meet again.

## After the Jubilee

I wrote this for *The Silver Jubilee Royal Variety Show* in 1977. My 12-minute spot came straight after the interval, when I guessed correctly and gloomily that latecomers would still be pouring in from the bars and toilets to take their seats. There had been enthusiastic celebration of the Silver Jubilee throughout the UK – street parties, processions and the ancient and, to me, peculiarly disturbing lighting of beacons along the hills. All this had been different and enjoyable, and I tried to bring some of it into the poem.

I remember two things about the day: one was the awful atmosphere in the London Palladium during rehearsals – the fear, the nerves, the occasional, spectacular clash of showbiz egos. It was a huge, memorable line-up with Bob Hope, Julie Andrews, the Muppets, Tommy Cooper and scores of famous faces. The other thing I remember is the strange division of concentration during the actual performance: of talking to the audience in front of me in the normal way, but also being acutely aware of the Royal Box up on my left, and the smudge of blue that was the Queen's dress.

I don't recall what else I declaimed during my 12 minutes, but I did include this.

## After the Jubilee

Don't play anything else on your squeeze box, Mother
To honour the Jubilee.
I daresay the Queen would enjoy it
But it has started grating on me.
Come and sit on this tattered old bunting,
Here's your tea in a Jubilee cup,
Don't play 'God save the Queen' for a minute
Or in other words, Mother … shut up.

Ah but how we rose to the occasion
With our patriotism and flags,
With our parties and fêtes and processions
And our Jubilee carrier bags.

How we planned for the local street party
With the sun beating down on our heads,
But unfortunately it rained on you and me
So we had it in Angus's shed.

But the dingy old street, how we decked it,
How the neighbours all chattered and talked
As they knocked the tin tacks in the Union Jacks
And the next day the whole lot had walked,
And the kiddies all rushed down to help us,
Who's to say industry never pays?
They wrote, 'Long may she reign' on the brickwork
And it did look, it poured down for days!

And the bonfires they lit in the village,
Well, we'll see nothing like it again,
And the only bonfire that burned brighter
Was the shock one up Arsonists Lane.
And we went on a torchlight procession,
We all bought special torches for that.
I held mine up high, proudly up in the sky,
And me shoulders got covered in fat.

So before you strike up again, Mother
Let me refill your Jubilee cup.
Me slab cake went down in the middle
But I've turned it the other way up.
The fireworks and fêtes are all over,
The street parties swept up and done.
Here's a message for Buckingham Palace,
Can we do it again? It was *fun*!

## To Make a Whale

Man is gloriously clever
Making intricate machines
And complicated gadgetry
And bigger runner beans
And journeys into space
With mighty rockets in the tail –
But when the last one's towed away
He couldn't make
   a whale.

## The Secretary's Song

Secretary is my trade,
Shorthand typist, second grade,
With me pad clutched in me hand a
Living breathing memoranda.
Like a ramrod on the seat,
I will sit up straight and neat.
With me feet placed close together,
I'll remark upon the weather,
But don't ask me more than that,
Because I haven't got the brain
To respond.

I find when seated in my chair,
With my conscientious stare,
Stabbing pains come in me eye for
What you write, I can't decipher.

But when I rush in with the teas,
I'll charm the birds right off the trees,
I'll run to do the washing up
And pick the fag ends from the cup
Until I hear the siren blow,
Then I'll just clock my card and go
Home.

I will not appear to choke
In conferences thick with smoke.
In vain I'll write the boring minute,
And assume some interest in it.
I won't elaborate the facts,
And I won't come to work in slacks
For they offend the royal eyeball
And that cannot be allowed at all,
For what's the point of women
If you cannot see their legs?

And when at last I'm seated by
The great typewriter in the sky,
Let me type the letters right,
In the morning and at night.
Let the Tipp-Ex grow on trees,
Let men's hands stay off me knees,
Let it be a place harmonic,
With no need for gin and tonic.
Thank you in anticipation
Of your favourable reply,
Craving your indulgence,
Yours sincerely,
Goodbye.

## *Where There's a Will*
### *... there's a sobbing relation*

All the family was gathered
To hear poor Grandad's will,
Fred was watching Alice,
And she was watching Bill,
He was watching Arthur,
Everywhere he went,
But specially at the cupboard,
Where Grandad kept the rent.

Outside on the patio,
The sliding door was closed,
And sitting in a chair
Was nephew John, his face composed.
He said, 'Me dear old Grandad,
I shall never see you more,'
And his sheets of calculations
Were spread across the floor.

Downstairs in the kitchen,
Sister Alice blew her nose,
Saying, 'He always was my favourite,
You *knew* that I suppose?
You couldn't have found a nicer man,
I've never loved one dearer.
I'd have come round *much* more often
If I'd lived just that bit nearer.'

Cousin Arthur sat alone
His eyes were wild and rash,
And desperately he tried to think
Where old folks hid their cash.
He'd thought about the armchair
And the mattress on the bed,
And he'd left his car at home
And booked a Pickford's van instead.

Then there were the bedroom floorboards
He'd studied every crack,
And twice, while dusting the commode,
He'd rolled the carpet back.
But he knew the others watched him
'You scavengers,' he cursed,
And every night he prayed,
'Don't let the others find it first.'

The day that Grandad's will was read,
It came up bright and clear,
The lawyer man looked round,
And said, 'Now then, are we all here?'
Someone shouted, 'Yes',
And someone else unscrewed his pen,
And someone sat upon his coat,
So he could not stand up again.

He carefully unfolded it
And wonderingly said,
'This is the shortest will
I ever will have read.'

He rolled a fag and carefully
Laid in a filter tip,
While beads of sweat they gathered
On Cousin Arthur's lip.

'It says: "Me dear relations,
Thank you all for being so kind,
And out beside the lily pond
You will surely find
The half a million pounds,
With which I stuffed me garden gnome,
Which I leave, with great affection,
To the Battersea Dogs' Home."'

## *The Vegetable Garden and the Runaway Horse*

In everybody's garden now
The grass has started growing.
Gardeners, they are gardening,
And mowers … they are mowing.
Compost heaps are rotting down,
And bonfires burning low,
So I took up me shovel,
And resolved to have a go.

I dug a patch of garden
That was not too hot or shady,
And not too large to tax
The constitution of a lady.
Everything which crossed my spade,
I flung it all asunder,
And that which I could not dig up,
I rapidly dug under.

And in my little plot,
I bravely laboured with the hoe,
Enthusiasm running rife,
I sprinted to and fro.
I stopped for nothing,
Not for food or drink or idle words,
Except a spotted dick
Someone had chucked out for the birds.

Imagine then my pleasure,
As it all came sprouting out,
I cast aside me dibber
And I swaggered round about,
But, alas, the gate
To which my garden was adjacent
Was open, and I never saw,
As up the path I hastened.

When I went down on Saturday,
A horse stood in my plot,
But nothing else stood in it,
For he'd eaten all the lot.
I said, 'Alas, my effort's wasted
And my garden wrecked.
Go away, you rotten horse,'
(Or words to that effect).

His hooves had crushed me lettuce,
And me radishes were mangled,
Broken canes were scattered
Where me runner beans had dangled.
The lovely shiny marrow
I'd been going to stuff and all,
The horse had broken off its stalk,
and kicked it up the wall.

Standing in the ruins
Of me Brussels sprouts and spinach,
I threw away me shovel
And I said, 'Well, that's the finich.

69

No early peas for me,
The birds can have them,
Or the mice might,
And if I want a cabbage,
Well, I'll see you down at Pricerite!'


## Not You, Basil

Basil he loved Ethel,
    In his heart there burned a flame.
Every night he gripped the sheets
    And whispered Ethel's name,
He saw her every morning
    And the breath caught in his throat.
He loved her in her summer dress
    And in her winter coat.

Each night the lovely Ethel,
    She came to him in a dream,
And lay reclining in the boat
    He rowed them in, upstream.
Her hand trailed in the water
    And she was a wondrous sight,
Saying, 'Basil! I can wait no more!
    Take me, tonight!'

But his love was unrequited.
    When he saw her every day,
She only said, 'How do,'

And hurried past him on her way
To catch the bus to work.
    Where every day from morn to eve
She gazed out of the window,
    Thinking of her true love. Steve.


Now Steve he ran a scrapyard.
    Once a week he knocked the door
And Ethel, she would open it,
    Saying, 'I know what you've come for!
Your rag and bones!' she cried,
    'And here they are, in this here sack,'
And she'd watch with heart a-flutter,
    As he heaved them on his back.


She never thought of Basil,
    Never knew that he was there.
From morn to eve, she thought of Steve,
    Her fingers, in his hair.
For Steve was rugged, like an oak,
    While Basil, like a skittle,
Had no physique, of which to speak,
    His muscles, they was little.


But his ardour never cooled
    And to himself he sadly said,
'If Ethel does not love me,
    I would just as soon be dead.
I'll knock upon her door,
    And say "I love you" and forsooth,
She can either take or leave me,
    But at least I'll know the truth.'

So he knocked upon her door
    And when she answered, he began:
'I know *someone* that you could make
    A Very Happy Man.'
Ethel gripped the doorpost,
    'Is it Steve? Oh can it be?'
And Basil, looking at her,
    He said, 'No, you fool, it's me.'

She said, 'Oh not *you*, Basil.
    I thought you'd come on Steve's behalf,
As though he'd see, a girl like me.'
    (She laughed a tragic laugh.)
She said, 'I interrupted you,
    What were you going to say?'
And Basil said, 'Don't matter,'
    And he coldly walked away.

Back in his house he primed his gun
    And placed it to his head,
'I die for Ethel, though my death'll
    Grieve her not,' he said.
He strained to press the trigger,
    But his courage upped and fled,
So he rushed out in the garden
    And he shot the cat instead.

## Little Lawrence Greenaway

Little Lawrence Greenaway,
He tended to digress.
He'd always tell you rather more
Instead of rather less.
Of wild exaggeration
He was never known to tire,
The facts became irrelevant,
In short, he was a liar.

He said, 'I'm in computers,
You name the sort, we've gottem,'
Whereas in fact he only
Screwed the castors on the bottom.
His claims they grew preposterous,
He couldn't understand
Why all of his companions,
Well, they laughed behind their hands.

One awful Monday morning,
He was sitting on the train,
He saw a great red-headed man
Come rushing down the lane.
Just as the train was leaving,
The man wrenched at the door
And stood above the passengers,
A mighty six foot four.

He opened up his great big mouth
And with a ghastly shout,
Hollered, 'Somewhere on this train's
The bloke who took my Missis out!'
Lawrence he was frightened,
Like a frightened little rabbit,
But he still said, 'It was me,'
You see, just through force of habit.

The great big man, he picked him up
Underneath the throat,
And helped him off the train,
Without returning for his coat.
With his head locked in a headlock
He was rushed off down the lane,
And little Lawrence Greenaway,
Was *never seen again.*

## The Spot Welder's Dream

I wish I was a pop star,
Colourful and brash,
With me earoles full of crotchets
And me wallet full of cash.
To hide me bit of acne
I'll stick sequins on me face,
Then I can do the vocals
And you can do the bass.
Yeah.

I can do the vocals,
But to whip them to a frenzy,
Seated at the organ
We'll have rockin' Bert McKenzie.
Now Bert's a lovely mover
But he tends to be a dunce,
When he's winking at the boppers,
He shuts both eyes at once.

I'll buy a cossack shirt
Split to the waist, in peacock red,
So me face will get them going
And me chest will knock them dead.
I'll wave me great long legs about
And wrap them round the mike.
I had a practice Saturday,
But I fell off me bike.

I'll get meself an agent
And a manager and all,
A bloke to drive the minibus,
And one to book the hall,
A musical arranger,
And a private record plugger,
So when we're in the charts,
Well, we shall all feel that much smugger.

And when we're doing a stand,
I'll come up quiet, to the mike,
I'll stick me pelvis out
And say, 'Right on ...' suggestive like.
I'll drive the women crazy,

They'll be in such a state.
And they'll scratch each other's eyes out,
Once I've had me teeth put straight.

Farewell Cradley Heath!
We're out upon the road to fame.
Farewell factory gates!
We're going to be a Household Name.
Good riddance Welding Shop,
And factory hooter every morn,
It's either me or Bert McKenzie,
But a Superstar is born.

# Pam Ayres and the Embarrassing Experience with the Parrot

We've always lived fairly close to the Cotswold Wildlife Park, a pleasant sort of zoo near Burford. One day I visited it with a friend, and this is more or less what happened, except that I have slightly embroidered the end.

Good ends to poems are tantalising and elusive things. They make or break what has gone before and are worth struggling with. People forget what a work of genius your ode may have been at the start if there is only a damp squib at the finish. I was always pleased with the end of this one, for its sense of full-circle completeness. Also, when I am performing this on stage I get the opportunity to portray a half-dead parrot swaying about on one leg, which is a great dramatic moment.

## Pam Ayres and the Embarrassing Experience with the Parrot

At the Cotswold Wildlife Park,
In the merry month of May,
I paid the man the money,
And went in to spend the day.
Straightway to the Pets Corner
I turned my eager feet,
To go and see the rabbits
And give them something to eat.

As I approached the hutches,
I was alarmed to see
A crowd of little yobbos,
'Ollerin' with glee.
I crept up close behind them
And weighed the scene up quick,
And saw them poke the rabbits
Poke them! ... with a stick!

'Get off you little devils!'
I shouted in their ear.
'Don't you poke them rabbits,
That's not why they are here!'
I must have really scared them,
In seconds they were gone,
And feeling I had done some good,
I carried on along.

Till up beside the Parrots Cage,
I stood to view the scene.
They was lovely parrots,
Beautiful blue and green,
In and out the nestbox,
They was really having fun,
Squawking out and flying about,
All except for one.

One poor old puffed-up parrot
Clung grimly to his perch,
And as the wind blew frontwards,
Backwards he would lurch.
One foot up in his feathers,
Abandoned by the rest,
He sat there, plainly dying,
His head upon his chest.

Well, I walked on down the pathway
And I stroked a nanny goat,
But the thought of parrots dyin'

Brought a lump into me throat.
I could no longer stand it
And to the office I fled.
Politely I began: 'S'cuse me,
Your parrot's nearly dead.'

Well, me and a curator,
In urgent leaps and bounds,
With a bottle of Parrot Cure,
Dashed across the grounds.
The dust flew up around us
As we reached the Parrots Pen,
And the curator he turned to me,
Saying, 'Which one is it then?'

You know what I am going to say:
He was not there at all,
At least, not where I left him.
No, he flew from wall to wall,
As brightly as a button
Did he squawk and jump and leap.
The curator was very kind,
Saying, 'I expect he was asleep.'

But I was humiliated
As I stood before the wire.
The curator went back
To put his feet up by the fire,
So I let the parrot settle,
And after a short search,
I found the stick the yobbos had,
And poked him off his perch.

# The Frogmarch

This is a story about frogs who each year, in order to breed, journey back to the pond in which they were hatched. To these small creatures, motorways are a major obstacle. St Giles' Fair used to arrive in Oxford each year on an endless convoy of slow vehicles.

## *The Frogmarch*

Move along the kerbstone there
And get back into line,
I *know* we've all been sitting here
Since twenty-five past nine.
I've been doing a traffic census,
And with no more hesitation,
I reckon by tonight,
We'll reach the central reservation.

Now, I don't want my tactics
Criticised no more today,
I realise that everybody
Knew a better way.
But you are simple country folk,
You do not often come
In contact with these heavy lorries
Rattling down to Brum.

I know that when compared
To boggy riverbanks and peat,
That M40 motorway

Was murder on your feet.
I also know that in the usual
Places where we sit,
We don't stand up to find
Our underneath stuck up with grit.

Course, life for us amphibians
Is getting very harsh.
Take the Witney by-pass,
It used to be a marsh.
They've irrigated all the land,
It's all gone to the dogs.
You get fantastic drainage,
But you don't get any frogs.

Still, keep your wits about you lads,
And before we're very much older,
We'll hop straight in the Promised Land,
And straight off this hard shoulder.
All the female frogs are there,
Tarting up the bower,
I'll give them that, they're very good,
That Sutton Coldfield shower.

Right then, watch the traffic,
'Cause I think I see a gap,
Wake old sleeping beauty up,
His head sunk in his lap,
Get your bits and pieces then,
Is everybody there?
Look left! ... Prepare to spring!
Oh, no ... here comes St Giles's Fair.

## *Sling Another Chair Leg on the Fire, Mother*

Sling another chair leg on the fire, Mother,
Pull your orange box up to the blaze,
Hold your poor old mittens out and warm them
In these inflationary days.
Sink your teeth into that dripping sandwich,
Flick the telly on to channel nine,
And if we get the sound without the picture,
Well, I'll kick it in the kidneys, one more time.

Come with me out to the empty garage,
We haven't been there for a week or more,
We'll bow our heads and gaze in silent homage
At the spots of oil upon the floor.
We'll think of when we had a motor car there,
Which used to take us out in rain or shine,
Before the price of petrol went beyond us,
And we'll make believe we kept it, one more time.

Fling another sausage in the pan, Mother!
We'll laugh away our worries and our cares,
But we'll never get a doctor after hours, Mother,
So for God's sake don't go falling down the stairs.
Toss another lentil in the soup, Mother!
And serve it up before the News at nine,
And if the GPO detector spots us,
Make believe we've got a licence, one more time.

There was a time we'd booked up for Ibiza,
We'd bought the suntan lotion and the clothes,
But we never got beyond the travel agent,
'Cause Court Line* organised the one we chose.
So knock the clouds of dust from off the brochure,
Wipe the 40-watt bulb free of grime,
Turn the dog-eared pages to Ibiza,
And we'll make believe we got there, one more time.

Pass me the hatchet and the axe, Mother!
Wipe away that sad and anxious frown,
What with these inflationary spirals,
It's *nice* to see the table falling down.
Your poor old shins will soon be good and mottled,
Once the flames get round that teak veneer,
And in the ring of warm and dancing firelight,
We'll smile and wish each other: Happy New Year.

*Court Line was a travel agent that had just gone
spectacularly bust.*

## Tiger, Tiger

The tiger that stalks through the night
Delivers a hideous bite
And there on his paws
Are razor-sharp claws
But apart from all that, he's all right!

## Mary Boggis Clark

Mary Boggis Clark from the top of Hatcher's End
Married Henry Crocker for a mentor and a friend.

She clung to Henry Crocker's arm when going for a stroll
For Mary Boggis Clark, she was a nervous little soul.

When they were recumbent in their feather marriage bed
Henry Crocker reached across to fondle Mary's head.

Imagine his surprise when Mary Clark began to scream
Explaining she had just been getting strangled in a dream.

And Mary Boggis Clark, she did not improve at all
From seeing faces in the dark and shadows on the wall.

Mary graduated to hallucinations better
And conjured up all kinds of things that came at night to
   get her;

And Henry's fond advances, they were rather brushed aside
And Henry's private yearnings – well, they went unsatisfied.

Often he would give her a preliminary peck
But the old familiar prickling on the back of Mary's neck

Would cause her to forget him crying, 'Henry! Henry! Hark!
I do believe there's someone creeping up here in the dark!'

Now very soon it all began to get on Henry's wick
He tired of Mary shouting, 'Henry! Henry! Wake up quick!'

He tired of groping half asleep at midnight round the room
In search of Mary's spectres as they rose up from the gloom.

He couldn't *hear* the bumping or the rattlers and bangers
That Mary said was spirits, phantoms, ghouls and
    doppelgangers.

Mary was so nervous it was difficult to leave her
Specially as beside the bed she kept the mutton cleaver.

With such frequent visitations Henry couldn't keep apace
And he watched in mute amazement as she cleavered round
    the place.

Mary went to the pictures just for something fresh to do
She found the film was *Werewolf in the Graveyard Meets
    Kung Fu.*

She didn't want to see it and her courage drained away
So she sat for ninety minutes trying to look the other way.

She came out of the pictures and her face was pale with fright
Darting nervous over-shoulder glances left and right.

She scuttled down the cobbles by the green and oily cut
Thinking she was safely home to Henry Crocker. But ...

She saw a figure moving on the water's other side –
A young man crept in view, his eyes were panicky and wide,

He stared at Mary Boggis Clark and jumped and cried, 'Oh no!'
And cringed beneath the street lamp in its pale and ghostly glow,

Mary strained her eyes to see, for all the lane was dim
She knew that she was scared but she was not as scared as him,

She stepped across the bridge and laid her hand upon his arm
For he was white and frightened ... but he had a certain charm.

'Good lady' cried the man, 'That you should see me in this state,
I never should have ventured from my home this far, this late;

For what handicaps my life and makes me eminently kickable
Is my fear of the supernatural and inexplicable.'

He said, 'I cannot walk the street or anywhere at all
Without this constant fear that round the back of every wall,

Listening for footsteps, crouched in menacing positions,
Are poltergeists and spooks and paranormal apparitions

And once outside my door, I found the sign, the Living Proof
For printed in the garden, there it was, the Cloven Hoof.

Although I will admit this theory was placed in doubt
For it coincided with the day me bullocks all got out,

Fear is what I live with of the most illogic kind,
Fear of being suddenly garotted from behind,

Fear of hooded phantoms that across the water float
To nod and wink and clench their bony fingers round me throat.'

Mary gazed about her and her face was white with joy
And she told him, 'You are not alone, I'm just the same ...
  my boy.

And they began to tremble now the wondrous truth was known
They trembled both at once and then he trembled on his own.

'Oh,' sighed Mary Boggis Clark with unrestrained relief,
'I am so greatly comforted, for it was my belief

That all through life alone I must these apparitions meet.
Come home with me and we'll throw Henry's things into
  the street.

I know he is my husband but alas! the outlook's grim
Statistics prove if someone's going to murder me ... it's *him*!'

'But I'm scared of my own shadow!' wailed the man and hung
  his head
But Mary Boggis Clark said, 'So am I' and they were wed!

And went on honeymoon where in the warm and sunny weather,
Hand in hand for life, they will be seeing things together.


### The Rat Resuscitation Rhyme

  I found a dead rat in our woodshed,
  I found it at quarter to eight,
  I tried to give it the kiss of life
  But I'd left it ten minutes too late.

## *Eat, Drink and Be Sick*

Well, Happy Christmas, Father,
Have I got a treat for you!
A pair of socks in bottle green
And one in navy blue.
I wrapped them round your after-shave
And put them by the tree
And wrote me name in biro
So you'd know they came from me.

Well yes, I'll have a mince pie please
And then I'll have a date
And then I'll crack a nut or two
And fling them in the grate,
And then I'll have a fig
And then perhaps a glass of wine
And then another two or three
To make me forehead shine.

One cold turkey sandwich
But a *small* one, understand.
Look, the meat's all falling out –
You got a rubber band?
Stoke the fire up, Father,
Ram the poker down the back,
Those taters in the ashes
Well, they've never looked so black!

I'll have a liqueur chocolate
With the crunchy sugar coat
That rattles round your teeth
And turns to gravel in your throat.
How nice the room looks, Mother,
With the tinsel round the walls,
I'll have an Advocaat then please,
Yes, that one there, the Bols.

Just one slice of Christmas cake
Then I shall have to run.
A tangerine then, if you *must* –
Just hold this Chelsea bun.
One glass of cherry brandy
No more crystal fruits for me!
Happy Christmas all!
I'm going home to have me tea!


## Miss Grundy and the Grand Hotel

Miss Grundy ran the Grand Hotel.
She called it grand but you couldn't tell
For it was very dark and drear
And dust stood thick on the chandelier.
The carpets once so plush and fine
Were full of holes and dust and wine
And the wallpaper embossed and plain
Had rolled itself back up again.

No music flowed in the marble halls,
No Gala Nights, Midsummer Balls,
Since the night that the Town and Country Planner
Tipped his beer down the old pianner.
No smile ever cracked the receptionist's face
But the smell of her nail polish oozed through
   the place
And, mixed with the fragrance of frying, it rose
To deal the hotel guests a punch on the nose.

Soon however the plot of land
Next door to the crumbling Grand
Came up for sale and folks heard tell
That there were plans for a new hotel.
Miss Grundy didn't care a jot
But sniffed, 'My regulars I've got.
They'd never dream of leaving here
They pay through the nose for the atmosphere!'

But they watched with wary eyes
As the new hotel blocked out the skies.
The receptionist, afire with dread,
Changed her nails from pink to red.
Not only had it H & C,
All mod cons and colour TV,
But taking shape along the corner
Was a brand new swimming pool ... and sauna!

Miss Grundy, deciding to put up a fight,
Took a broom to the chandelier one night
And so that people could get up late
Didn't *stop* breakfast till quarter to eight.

To enable the music and dancing to start
She stood up one night and sang 'Heart of my Heart',
She hung up pictures of Highland cattle
But Miss Grundy alas fought a losing battle.

For the guests at the Grand Hotel saw the light
And all tunnelled out under cover of night
Under the room where Miss Grundy snored,
Where the mousetraps guarded the skirting board,
Into the warmth of the one next door,
The swimming pool and the carpet floor,
While outside stirring in the chilly breeze
Miss Grundy's sign read 'Vacancies'.

## *Take Me Back to Old Littlehampton*

I didn't *want* this holiday
I know I shan't enjoy it.
If I think of any way to hamper yours
Then I'll employ it.
I didn't like the journey
And I don't like our hotel
And I wish I'd stayed at home
That would have done me very well.

No! I am *not* going swimming,
Not with my infected ear,
Not with all those half-dressed women
Running up and down, no fear.
I'll just sit here in the bedroom
Oh and pull the curtains, do
For the sun inflames me headache.
It's quite all right for you!

You go and have a lovely time
Don't think of me at all.
I've got me English paper
You go out and have a ball,
You go and have a rave up!
Go on! And have a fling!
Don't come for me at dinner time,
I couldn't eat a thing.

Last night I ate that gastro-enteritis on a plate.
I thought I'd make it to the Ladies'
But no, I was too late.
Go on! Enjoy your dinner!
Have the olive oil and wine!
But buy some Alka Seltzer:
I shan't give you one of mine!

I could have been at home now
Sitting watching the TV
With me hair all washed and set
And with the cat sat on me knee.
I can't use me heated rollers
For the volts are up the creek
And the bath's all full of sand –
I haven't had one for a week!

Still, it's all right, no it's lovely,
And we saved up for a year.
Dear Mother, having a lovely time
I wish that you were here.
How I let myself be talked
Into a fortnight I dunno,
Still you go out – enjoy it!
One week down. And one to go.

## ailway Carriage Couple

ale, when I was a girl, there was one couple verted railway carriage. It was very black but it had ..... arch at the entrance, and it was covered all over with more ros... and climbing plants. It looked like a very well-loved home.

### The Railway Carriage Couple

Our home's a railway carriage
And it cannot be denied
That you might describe our dwelling
As a little bit on the side
Yet it has the odd advantages
Where other housing fails
And we're on the straight and narrow
So we can't go off the rails!

Our decor is original
It's simple but it's good
With little plaques screwed on the wall
That give the type of wood
And up above the headrest
Of the seat marked number five
Is a photograph of Cheddar Gorge
In case we don't arrive.

Yes we're the railway carriage couple
With the long drive at the front
Or it might be at the back
If we feel like a change, and shunt
We're a little isolated
But if ever I get bored
And feel like communicating
I stand up and pull the cord.

I don't do much entertaining,
It's too cramped, you see, by far
For dining graciously
Because it's not a buffet car,
So we eat out in the corridor,
My husband doesn't care
But I like to face the engine
Even though it isn't there.

Of course there is a certain problem
Which we have and always will
In that we cannot use the toilet
While the train is standing still
So we built one just beside us

And we glazed it in with glass
The first time my husband used it
He came back and said 'First Class!'

We have a little garden
We don't buy much in the town
You can see us any evening
Raking clinker up and down
You might see us in our door
If you don't travel by too fast
And we'll let down two holes in the leather strap
And wave as you go past.


## The Stuffed Horse

There was a stuffed horse what had died,
And the townspeople stood it with pride
On a plinth in the Square,
And the shoppers went there,
And sat, for a rest, by its side.

Beneath the stuffed horse was a plaque,
Only vandals had painted it black,
What told of the deed
Of the glorious steed,
And the General, what rode on its back.

The bold horse, with never a care,
Had ducked cannonballs in the air,
And stood to the end

By the General, his friend,
Which was why he was put in the Square.

Well, his tail it was stuck out with wire,
And paint made his nostrils afire,
And his bold eye of glass
Gazed upon concrete grass,
When he met with his fate, what was dire.

This night from the shadows a-fidget
Extended a beckonin' digit.
A voice whispered, 'Right,'
And into the night
Rushed ten men, a saw and a midget.

They lay by the horse with no word,
And the soft sound of sawing was heard.
In silence, all night,
Stuffin' flew left and right,
And into a sack was transferred.

When the church clock struck quarter to four,
Ten men ran away, and a saw.
But the midget, my friend,
Was not there at the end,
He was with his companions no more.

When morning it broke on the Square,
You would never have known they'd been there,
For the horse gazed away,
Like the previous day,
Just sniffin' the spring in the air.

But walkin' across to the spot
Came two ladies whose feet had grown hot.
They sat on the ground,
And one got out a pound,
Saying: 'Here's that quid I owed to you, Dot.'

From the back of the stuffed horse's throat
Came a hand and it snatched the pound note.
With the hand, and the cash,
The jaws shut with a clash,
And the horse gazed away with a gloat.

The lady was helped off to bed.
'I thought they liked hay, dear,' she said.
No one listened, of course,
For it was a stuffed horse
What never required to be fed.

But it happened again, the next day,
When a vicar had sat down to pray,
He said, 'Lord, bless my flock,'
When a great lead-filled sock
Took his senses, and wallet, away.

But by now the long arm of the law
Started pickin' up pieces of straw,
What might have been nothin'
But could have been stuffin',
And random observers, they saw.

That the stuffed horse's eye, though of glass,
Had seemed to be watchin' them pass

And sometimes would blink
Or give you a wink,
As if to say, 'Step on my grass.'

Hadrian of the Yard, he was called,
He was like Fabian, only bald.
He said, 'I'll be an idiot,
If there's not a midgiot
Inside of the stuffed horse installed.'

And indeed, that great sleuth, he was right.
By Caesarean, they caught him that night,
With ten men and a saw,
He had broken the law
Illegal entry, all right.

But tragic indeed was the scene
In the place where the stuffed horse had been.
Bandy-legged and defaced,
He had to be replaced,
By an ordinary bust of the Queen.

# The Car Wash Black and Blues

I never take my car to the car wash if I can help it. It's not that I wouldn't like it to be sparkling clean with a deep, fathomless shine, but rather that I am uncomfortable, verging on claustrophobic, shut inside a car as it goes through the car-wash process.

I think they are better lit now. The early ones I tried seemed to be housed in the gloomiest of long black buildings. It was always nerve-racking to line up the car properly so that it was the correct distance from the rolling black brushes. A surly man used to gesture at you, drawing you into the tunnel; then he would make a run for it and leave you on your own. Slowly, the great menacing brush would start to revolve and take on a life of its own, swinging down from the ceiling and flattening grotesquely on the windscreen amid a deafening drumming and slashing of water. Other brushes would appear and mob you from the sides. I was always afraid they were trying to get in. Once I had a car with little quarter-light windows and stupidly forgot to close one. It was madly slapped in all directions as freezing water snaked in, and I frantically tried to cover the hole with my flattened hand.

I wrote this ages ago, in about 1978, but I still feel the same and offer it as my excuse for driving an exceedingly grubby-looking car.

## The Car Wash Black and Blues

Oh Dad, oh please don't send me down the Car Wash
Just like you send me every Friday night,
For on seeing the mechanical contrivance
I find that I am overcome with fright.
I put my fifty pence into the slot, Dad,
And as the mechanism starts to go,
The last thing that I see before the darkness
Is the wash attendant saying, 'Cheerio.'

And it's black, Dad, black as night inside the Car Wash,
And every time I realise too late
That the wireless aerial's not in the socket
And before my eyes it scribes a figure eight.
I know it's quick, Dad, speedy and efficient,
Them brushes clean the car from head to feet
But they also get the windscreen wipers, Daddy
And flick them half a mile across the street.

Them rubbers, Dad, they're slapping at the window;
I know they're supposed to make the paintwork gleam
But I am thinking, Dad, in all the racket
Will anybody *hear* me when I scream?
It's proper claustrophobic in the Car Wash,
Them brushes, Dad, are sinister and black.
If the front one doesn't lift the lid and get you,
Another one is rolling up the back.

You haven't got a coward for a son, Dad,
For all the times my back you've gaily slapped,
It's just that with the Car Wash coming at me
I sort of get the feeling that I'm trapped.
And all that drumming, Dad, it isn't water
It's hot wax spraying all around the place;
One day I left the quarterlight ajar, Dad,
And hot wax spattered all across my face.

Oh Dad, don't let us patronise the Car Wash
Let us use our old-fashioned plan,
Washing it ourselves on Sunday morning
With a squirt of Fairy Liquid in the can.
Don't send me down the Car Wash any more, Dad,
Send my sister, send my cousin Alf,
Send someone insensitive and stupid
Or alternatively, drive it there yourself!

## I Am a Cunnin' Vending Machine

I am a cunnin' vending machine
Lurkin' in the hall,
So you can't kick me delicate parts
I'm bolted to the wall.
Come on! Drop in your money,
Don't let's hang about,
I'll do my level best to see
You don't get nothing out.

I sees you all approachin',
The fagless and the dry,
All fumblin' in your pockets,
And expectant in the eye.
I might be in your place of work,
Or on the High Street wall.
Trust in me! In theory,
I cater for you all.

Within these windows I provide
For every human state,
Hunger, night starvation,
And remembering birthdays late.
Just read the information,
Pop the money in – that's grand,
And I'll see absolutely nothing
Ever drops down in your hand.

I might be at your swimming bath,
And you'd come, cold and wet,
With some money in your hand,
Some hot soup for to get.
And as you stand in wet
Anticipation of a sup,
I will dispense the soup,
But I will not dispense the cup.

And then it's all-out war,
Because you lost your half-a-nicker.
Mighty kicks and blows with bricks
Will make me neon flicker,
But if you bash me up,
So I'm removed, me pipes run dry,
There's no way you can win,
I'll send me brother by and by.

Once there was friendly ladies,
Years and years before,
Who stood with giant teapots,
Saying, 'What can I do you for?'
They'd hand you all the proper change,
And pour your cup of tea,
But they're not economic so ...
Hard luck! You're stuck with me.

## Clamp the Mighty Limpet

I like the idea of an obstreperous limpet, one that studies you threateningly from under the edge of his shell and thinks warlike thoughts. I used to imagine that they just sat on their rock, year in, year out, and didn't do much. In fact my husband once said I had the brain of a limpet, which I took to be an unusual insult. One day I happened to mention this on the radio.

In response I received a letter from a marine biologist who had been listening. He said I should not be at all put out by my husband's comment because in fact the limpet is a highly resourceful and admirable critter. Apparently, the limpet moulds himself to one particular spot and waits to be submerged when the tide comes in. Once under water, he releases his suction pad and sets off at a smart pace, scuttling over the rocks on various bits of limpet business. However, and this is the nitty-gritty, as soon as the limpet senses that the tide is receding, he can somehow navigate back to his original, exact spot and there orientate and clamp himself to precisely the same place. Therefore, said the marine biologist, the brain of a limpet was not a thing to be sniffed at, and I should ignore my husband. Which I usually do.

## Clamp the Mighty Limpet

I am Clamp the Mighty Limpet
I am solid, I am stuck,
I am welded to the rockface
With my superhuman suck.
I live along the waterline
And in the dreary caves.
I am Clamp the Mighty Limpet!
I am Ruler of the Waves.

What care I for the shingle,
For the dragging of the tide,
With my unrelenting sucker
And my granite underside?
There's only one reward
For those who come to prise at me
And that's to watch their fingernails
As they go floating out to sea.

Don't cross *me*, I'm a limpet,
Though it's plankton I devour.
Be very, very careful
I can move an inch an hour!
Don't you poke or prod me
For I warn you – if you do
You stand there for a fortnight
And I'll come and stick on you!


## The Sea Shell

Don't 'ee fret no more, my darlin' Alice,
Don't 'ee cry and sorrow, my old dear,
Don't 'ee watch the lane for our son Arnold,
Lost upon the sea this fourteen year.
Let a smile play on your lips again, Alice,
Fourteen years you've worn the widow's drab,
And get your ear away from that great sea shell:
*Nobody* hears the ocean in a crab.

## *Arthur Dan Steely, the Novelty Act*

Arthur Dan Steely, the Novelty Act,
Stood in the hallway: his cases were packed.
He called to his wife saying, 'Leave you I must'
And she clung to the door knob and laughed fit to bust.
He straightened his shoulders and took up his case
Taking a last look around the old place,
He took in the dirt and the cracks and the holes
And said, 'When I come back I'll come in a Rolls.'

He opened the door and he walked down the street,
And behind him his wife couldn't stand on her feet.
She laughed and she laughed, she was tickled to death;
And her face ran with tears and she gasped for her breath.
But Arthur Dan Steely, the Novelty Act,
Sat on a bus and his pride was intact,
Mentally checking the props he had taken,
His faith in his talent was firm and unshaken.

They were holding auditions for Unusual Acts:
Arthur Dan Steely had read all the facts.
He signed at the Stage Door, then boldly beneath
Wrote: Arthur Dan Steely for Tunes on the Teeth!
Yes! It was true! It was his Act alone!
He'd learnt all its foibles as each tooth had grown.
Now, perfectly tuned from the north to the south
They were like a whole orchestra packed in his mouth.

# The Works

There were singers and dancers and acrobats there
And a director sat in a director's chair
And Arthur Dan Steely he took off his 'mac
And selected a dignified seat, at the back.
The singers did sing and the acrobats leap
And the director peacefully went off to sleep.
And Arthur Dan Steely grew nervous and sat
Patiently waiting and twisting his hat.

At last the address system booming and cracked
Said, 'Arthur Dan Steely, the Novelty Act!'
He took up the pencil and switched on the tape
And walked on the stage with his mouth all agape.
He graciously bowed to the people within
And, to show them his instruments, flashed them a grin.
He tuned up a bit in the way of great bands
And everyone covered their mouths with their hands.

Then the music began! It was just like a spur!
He shot round the stage and his feet were a blur,
Tapping above and tapping beneath
And flakes of enamel, they shot off his teeth.
The music was frenzied, he gave it his all!
He gave them Scott Joplin and 'After the Ball'.
The Director woke up and looked, it was odd
For he covered his eyes up and said, 'Oh, Good God!'

He had just reached the point where, to give them a laugh,
He bit that particular pencil in half
When he stopped in his tracks. He was shocked and perplexed
Oh, surely he hadn't heard someone shout 'Next!'

Yes he had! An assistant just waved him away,
As he'd wave at a fly on a hot summer's day.
And onto the stage came a juggling troupe,
The Dinner Plate Whirlers from Old Guadeloupe.

Arthur Dan Steely, his case on his lap,
Sat on the omnibus taking a nap.
The shiny black tyres, they whined underneath.
But Arthur was shattered and so were his teeth.
He trudged up his street in the fast fading light;
His wife, who'd stopped laughing, said, 'You're late tonight.
I poured you a Guinness to drown all your sorrow –
We'll just have to hope you're discovered tomorrow!'

## Will Anybody Marry Me?

Will anybody marry me?
I would not cost him dear
I am in perfect nick
And good condition for the year
He would not have to be a Mr World
Built like Fort Knox
For I would do the plastering
And saw up all the blocks.

Will anybody marry me?
I would be awful sweet
I'd let him knock me glasses off
And kick them down the street

And I would not be a nagger
Saying 'Will you paint the pelmet?'
And if he was a fireman
I would never dent his helmet.

Concerning older girls
Our inhibitions have all gone
And me dad's an electrician
So I'd really turn him on
Now I cannot give my telephone
That's hazardous I know
But if anyone will have me
It is Bognor 410.

## *I Fell for a Black and White Minstrel*

I fell for a black and white minstrel,
He tickled me under the chin,
What I wanted to say was 'You go away'
But I actually said 'Oh ... come in'
In a minute I was captivated,
I had not a second to think,
What I could not erase, as I gazed in his face,
Was 'What does he look like ... pink!'

We went to his lodgings in Clapham,
Ostensibly we went for tea,
Only I kept on sort of looking at him,
And he kept sort of looking at me,

And the thing with a black and white minstrel,
They're not like a man who is clean,
If you've covered your chest, with a pearly white vest,
You can very soon see where he's been.

He sang me 'Oh dem Golden Slippers!'
He danced me a pulsatin' dance,
With his muscular thighs, and his white-circled eyes,
A maiden like me stood no chance,
He flung off his gold lamé jacket,
And likewise his silver top hat,
He cared not a fig, as he tore off his wig,
And I'm telling you no more than that.

But too early the traffic grew louder,
And I knew that it had to be dawn,
I reached for me black and white minstrel,
But me black and white minstrel had gorn,
I sat all alone in the morning,
Not wanting to understand,
That I had been only a plaything,
I was only a pawn … in his hand.

To this day I still cherish the pillow,
Where my black and white minstrel did lie,
There was one little place, where he laid his black face,
And one where he laid his white eye,
Me black and white minstrel has left me,
Gorn! with never Goodbye,
But my heart will be with him in Clapham,
Till the waters of Swannee, run dry.

# Please Will You Take Your Children Home Before I Do Them In?

I wrote this uncharitable piece shortly after I bought my first home. I was very proud of it and took great trouble over hanging pictures, artfully arranging flowers and placing delicate china ornaments on low shelves. Then, having added the last finishing touch, I invited my friend to stay. She arrived with her two young children.

An earthquake could not have rocked my home more. The pictures fell shattered from the walls, the ornaments and flowers went west, the dog was strangulated; I was dumbstruck. Of course, once I had children of my own, I could see that this behaviour was pretty much the norm, and it was me who was at fault for not putting away dainty things. At the time, though, on the day they went home I waved off the little family, closed the front door and in the beautiful ensuing silence sat down and wrote this.

## *Please Will You Take Your Children Home Before I Do Them In?*

Please will you take your children home
Before I do them in?
I kissed your little son
As he came posturing within.
I took his little jacket
And removed his little hat
But now the visit's over
So push off you little brat.

And don't think for a moment
That I didn't understand
How the hatchet he was waving
In his grotty little hand
Broke my china teapot
That I've always held so dear –
But would you mind removing him?
And take his jungle spear.

Of course I wasn't angry
As I shovelled up the dregs,
I'm only glad the teabags
Didn't scald his little legs.
I'm glad he liked my chocolate cake
I couldn't help but laugh
As he rubbed it in the carpet ...
Would he like the other half?

He guzzled all the orange
And he guzzled all the Coke –
The only thing that kept me sane
Was hoping he might choke.
And then he had a mishap,
Well, I couldn't bear to look,
Do something for your Auntie little sunshine ...
Sling your hook.

He's playing in the garden
He's throttled all the flowers,
Give the lad a marlinspike
He'll sit out there for hours.

## The Works

I've gathered my insecticides
And marked them with their name
And put them up where children
Couldn't reach them. That's a shame.

Still he must have liked my dog
Because he choked her half to death,
She'll go out for another game
Once she's caught her breath.
He rode her round the garden
And he lashed her with his rope
She's never bitten anyone
But still, we live in hope.

He's kicked the TV now!
I like to see it getting booted
Kick it one more time son
You might get electrocuted!
Yes, turn up the volume,
Twist the knobs, me little treasure
And when the programme's over
There's the door. It's been a pleasure.

## The Dreadful Accident
## with the Kitchen Scissors

I gave my lovely teddy bear a haircut,
For Mother she had sent me for a trim
And really, I felt that much better for it
I thought that I would do the same for him.
I picked him up and grabbed the kitchen scissors,
'Just a snip or two old bear,' I said,
But I find I was not meant to be a barber,
For accidentally, I cut his head.

I do not criticise the man who stuffed him,
He had to do it thoroughly no doubt,
But I wish he had not stuffed the head so solid
Then I could stop the stuffing coming out.

I've had to wrap me bear's head in a turban
Well, he's been dressed up like it for a week.
Mum asked me, 'What's he got that round his head for?'
I said, 'It's a turban Mummy – he's a Sikh!'

But how long can I keep up the deception?
Where his face was plump it's sunken in
And though he's very hard across the forehead
He's turning very soft around the chin!
I haven't dared to look beneath his turban,
I know it's just a mass of coloured foam,
And Mother's started looking very puzzled
As she picks up bits of it around the home.

And Auntie Greta's coming here for dinner
And she's the one who gave the bear to me
And that is when my crime will be uncovered
For I know that he won't stand much scrutiny.
Oh Mother, Auntie Greta, I'm so sorry!
I *tried* to sew his head up, I tried hard!
But as I said, they stuffed his head so tightly
That every stitch has stretched out half a yard!

I'm waiting by the door for Auntie Greta,
I rammed poor Teddy underneath the quilt,
And every time a car stops by our gateway
Both me knees start knocking from the guilt.
She's bound to say, 'Now where's that lovely Teddy?'
And his head's all caving in ... What shall I *do*?
Oh Crikey, here it is, a blue Marina ...
Oh, Hello Auntie Greta ... how are you?

## Sam and the Paraffin Man

Sam came home one evening,
The same as all his life,
To find the paraffin man
Had absconded with his wife.
Her coat from off the hanger
And her bootees from the stair
Had vanished, disappeared,
And furthermore, they were not there.

He came in through the kitchen,
The place was cold and still.
He tiptoed up the stairs,
In case his missis might be ill.
But nagging doubts they gathered,
Till what really did him in
Was, all across the landing,
He could smell the paraffin.

He took his knuckleduster
And he pressed it on his fist,
He also took a brick
In case the knuckleduster missed.
He set off down the darkened road,
Towards the caravan
Where he believed his missis
She was with another man.

'Oh, the paraffin man, is it?'
Muttered Sam at every stride.
A little bird had told him
How the lorry stayed outside,
How all the neighbours down the street
Joined in the fun and games,
And said with all that oil,
Sam's house might well burst into flames.

He came upon the caravan,
His temper running riot,
But even he had to agree
The place was very quiet.
But then it quickly dawned on Sam,
This silence was a trick!
So he rushed up to the fanlight
And he hit it with a brick.

'Come out here with my missis!'
He bellowed at the door.
'I've heard about your lorry,
Parked outside two hours and more.'
The caravan door opened
To reveal a woman's head,
And then a woman's nightdress,
For she'd just got out of bed.

She said, 'I'm not the paraffin man,
But I am one of his daughters.
You look so worried, Sam,
Can I pour oil on troubled waters?'

She beckoned in the caravan
And Sam stepped up so quick.
Enraptured by her beauty,
He forgot to drop the brick.

Now unbeknown to Sam,
His faithless wife, she had not fled,
But with the paraffin man,
She was hiding in his shed.
She crept up to the window,
Though she had to kneel and crouch,
And saw her husband Samuel
Suffocating on the couch.

She took a pail of water
And she flung it in the door,
Just for to cool his ardour,
Only that and nothing more.
Too late she realised
That it was paraffin she threw,
And they all went up to Heaven
On a cloud of Esso Blue.

But on a winter's evening,
If your feet are less than quick,
You might smell an oily fragrance,
You might see a ghostly wick,
You might hear the distant rumble
Of a passing caravan,
For things that passion can't ignite,
Paraffin can.

## *A Tale of Two Settees*

It was down at the furniture warehouse,
As I wandered one morning in May,
To buy a settee for the woodworm
Had eaten me old one away.
It was there in a flash that I saw him
In front of the chipboard veneer.
His Levis and shirt were covered in dirt
And he had a gold stud in his ear.

I did not let on that I'd seen him
Oh no, for I played hard to get,
Deliberating by the vinyl
And stroking the uncut moquette.
But he casually walked over to me
And seductively murmured, 'Oi, Oi,'
And there in the furniture warehouse
I said, 'Well … you are a tall boy!'

He said, 'Can I be of assistance?
Or offer a little advice?
Now if it's a sofa you're after
Well, this one's especially nice,
Upholstered in sultry black leather
And done round the edges in chrome,
And I know it withstands shocking treatment
For I happen to have one at home.'

Oh I know it was wrong but I liked him;
I knew he would lead me astray.
And yet as the sun caught his earring
I heard myself saying, 'Okay.'
When he asked me to go to the pictures
And ignoring the customers' glares
I said, 'Is it Studio One then or Two?'
He said, 'Studio Three. That's upstairs.'

So I met him that Saturday evening
I went all dressed up in me prime.
He brought me a fragile white orchid
And a drink on a stick at half time.
He bought me a carton of popcorn
He smiled as I prised up the lid.
'Oh thank you,' I said to him softly
And he laughed and said, 'Stick with me ... kid.'

We went for a Chinese and there in the dark
To the clang of the Chinese top ten,
'Your beauty,' he said, 'has gone to my head
With the sweet and sour pork.' Oh and then
He said, 'Darlin' it's wrong, but I'll ask you,
Oh, make all my cravings complete,
Instead of just buying a sofa
Why don't you invest in a suite?'

# The Ballad of Bill Spinks' Bedstead

I bought a three-bedroom terraced house in 1977. It was in Abingdon Road, Standlake, close to a local pub picturesquely named The Golden Balls. It was the first home I ever owned, cost £11,500, came with a small garden and garage, and I absolutely loved it. Having previously rented a furnished flat, I had very little furniture of my own, just one cane stool fashioned in the shape of a lobster pot and not much else. I needed a bed.

I was now working in the world of television, and people were different. These folk were no plodders. Suddenly I was among creative media types, arty advertising boffins, people who knew what was what. One day I told my new friends that I was looking for a bed. The decision was unanimous. There was only one place for me to go. It was fashionable; it was witty; it was essential. They gave me the address on a piece of paper, and I obediently went.

I found the shop in some unknown part of London, and it was like nothing I had ever seen before. Our family usually went to Courts in Swindon. I went awkwardly in and gawped at the beds on offer. One had a headboard made to look like a piano keyboard, the kind of thing you might imagine occupied by Liberace or Elton John. Another bed was made like a swan with great wings rising up at the sides. These were flamboyant creations, like theatrical sets. I only wanted a four-drawer divan. There was no point in even mustering the courage to ask the price, and I left empty-handed. However, the sight of these lavish, flight-of-the-imagination beds gave me the idea for 'The Ballad of Bill Spinks' Bedstead'.

At the time I wrote this, it was becoming popular for groups of young men to go off on the newly available cheap Spanish holidays. A very popular souvenir for them to bring home was a made-up bullfighting poster. This looked authentic, giving the date and venue, and listing the names of lesser Spanish matadors taking part. However, when it came to proclaiming the top of the bill, the star of the show, this would turn out to be the English holiday-maker himself, his name writ large on the poster, as if he had actually taken part. These things must have been printed by the thousand and were brought home as a suitably foreign-flavoured joke to be pinned up in the local pub.

Bill Spinks, having such a poster on his bedroom wall, was following the trend of the day.

### The Ballad of Bill Spinks' Bedstead

Bill Spinks gazed round his bedroom
From the ceiling to the floor,
To the ancient bullfight poster
With him as the matador.
And something was amiss
That he could not put into words
But in simple language it was this:
He didn't get the birds.

He supposed his furniture
Would never fill a bird with joy:
The bedside cupboard cobbled up
In 'Woodwork' as a boy;
And flapping at the window
Was a tired bit of chintz,
And round the light switch on the wall
Were dirty fingerprints.

Bill Spinks, propped up with pillows,
Gazed about in deep depression –
The bed was half the trouble
It gave such a bad impression.
You could try no acrobatics here
And if by chance you should
The springs played such a melody
It woke the neighbourhood.

It had no padded headboard –
This was wooden, from his mother.
It was eighteen inches high one side
And two foot on the other.
The rocky, flocky mattress
Though its origins were dim
Had crippled seven generations
And was hard at work on him.

So Bill Spinks formed a plan
He went methodically about it:
He wrote himself a shopping list
Got up and went without it.
But if he had remembered it
The first instruction read:
Cash your National Savings
And buy yourself a bed!

He stepped into the shop
He had his breakfast in his hand,
It was a mutton sandwich
Tied up with a rubber band.

And there he bought a bed
Which was fantastic beyond words:
A bed to revolutionise his life
(and get the birds!).

Oh, but what a bed it was
Upholstered all in damson suede,
And when you pressed a button
All the quadrasonics played,
And set into the headboard
Ringed in chromium and cork
A clock told you the time
In Bulawayo and New York.

It had an Operations Centre
With a neon-lit console
With a phone correctly placed
To get your finger in the hole.
A button for the video,
And if you pressed another
It made a cup of tea
And showed a picture of your mother.

126

If you pulled a hidden lever
The electric lights all blinked
And a rubber blow-up woman
Stripped off all her clothes and winked.
And in the dead of night
If you should feel the need to go
A claw came out from under
And it offered you the po.

So with the bed installed
Bill Spinks went looking for a mate.
The bed puffed up his ego
Which had flagged so much of late.
He went off down the disco
And the atmosphere was nice
With everybody spitting –
And a few had thrown up twice.

Yes, the Throttlers and the Wrenchers
They were both on stage together,
Punishing their instruments
In glossy wet-look leather.
But it was hard to tell
Because they'd all got so entrenched
Who was doing the throttling
And who was getting wrenched!

But he saw Ms Grippo Millet –
She'd have been the best girl there
If it wasn't for her face, her feet,
Her figure and her hair.

She was the most exquisite creature
Bill Spinks had ever seen:
Half her hair was purple
And the other half was green.

And he danced with Grippo Millet
From the moment that they met
While the Wrenchers' and the Throttlers'
music grew more frenzied yet.
And Bill Spinks said, 'Oh Grippo!
Come with me and spend the night.'
And Grippo Millet said, 'I'm not like that you know ...
    All right.'

Meanwhile in Bill Spinks' house
The bed was silent and aggrieved.
*This* was not the kind of setting
For which it had been conceived.
The rain blew in the window
And it pattered on the suede
And the bed thought of the showroom
And it wished it could have stayed.

It could hear Bill Spinks and Grippo
As they carried on below –
The bed sensed what was coming next
And didn't want to know.
But luckily it had
Beneath the damson suede protection
A 90-horsepower engine
With twin carbs and fuel injection.

Now Bill had coaxed his Grippo
To the bottom of the stair
And his hands were turning purple
As he rubbed them through her hair,
And just as Grippo Millet
Was responding to his touch
A sound came from above them
As the bed let in the clutch!

Well it was weary to the mattress
Of the mean and dingy view,
So it slapped itself in gear
And went to look for somewhere new.
It stunned Bill Spinks in passing
With a po jab from the right
And with all the covers flapping
Disappeared into the night.

Grippo watched the apparition
'What the hell was that?' she said,
Bill Spinks, his head still ringing,
Said, 'I think it was me bed.'
So she stayed to comfort Bill
Because he seemed at such a loss
And the bed has found a lovely home
In a house outside Kings Cross.

## The Husband's Lament or
## Well, You Certainly Proved Them Wrong

The flowers round our garden gate
Are strangled now with nettles,
The caterpillars got the leaves,
The road dust got the petals,
There's cracks across the asphalt path,
And the dusty wind do blow,
I know they say 'domestic bliss',
But I dunno. ...

There's trikes chucked on the garden
And there's writing on the wall,
The kids have smashed the wash house
With their little rubber ball.
The paint's peeled off the woodwork,
And the gutter's sagging fast,
I bodged it up last autumn,
But ... it didn't last.

And in our shattered living room,
The telly's on the blink,
There's fag ends in the saucers,
And peelings in the sink,
There's holes burned in the carpet,
Where it smouldered half the night.
'A Woman's Work is Never Done'
And you certainly proved that right.

There's barnacles in the goldfish bowl
And curlers on the floor,
The budgie's out the window
And the woodworm's in the door.
The leaves fell off the rubber plant,
The leg fell off the bed,
The smiles fell off our faces
And the back fell off the shed.

And *you*, who I adored,
One look and I knew I was falling,
You stole away my heart,
Beneath the moon and that tarpaulin,
It *can't* be you beside me,
With your tights so full of holes,
Chewing through your supper,
All them piccalilli rolls.

We've been together twenty years today,
And there's a moral,
We have no conversation,
So we never have a quarrel,
We hardly see each other,
So we never have a fight,
For 'Silence it is Golden'
And we've certainly proved that right.

## *Dear Lord Lichfield*

Dear Lord Lichfield, I am writing in despair,
Like you, I'm a photographer of genius and flair,
I know my subject thoroughly, I've studied hard and long,
And I beg of you to tell me what it is I'm doing wrong.

I recently selected, having waded through the hype,
A sophisticated camera of the Instamatic type,
With comprehensive settings, sunny, changeable or mist,
And a leather-look device that lets you swing it from
   your wrist.

I photographed the Queen as she drove past, I do not carp,
I *know* Her Majesty was blurred but was the background
   ever sharp
I sent it to the Palace with my number and my name,
And waited by the phone but no commission ever came.

Then I thought I'd specialise in birds of marsh and bog,
Imagine my delight to see a heron on a log,
I crept about it stealthily, I snapped it fore and aft,
But it was plastic from the pet shop and the kids went
   nearly daft.

My photographs are blighted and to cap it all this week,
Another lot fell short of the perfection that I seek,
With unexpected shadows and alarmingly, on some,
An apparition almost like a monumental thumb.

This summer, for a special treat, with no regard for cash,
I sallied forth and bought myself an electronic flash,
So all my subjects can relax and never have a shred
Of doubt that on the photograph their eyes will all be red.

Apertures and shutters are no mystery to me,
I know my lens Lord Lichfield like you know your ABC
With my extensive knowledge of all photographic lore,
Frankly I'm amazed I haven't toppled you before.

So maybe as you languish with a flunkey at your arm,
You being a Lord of character and undisputed charm,
In raising up a noble silver chalice to your lips,
You'll recall your fellow cameraman and send a couple of tips.

## Puppy Problems

As soon as I started working for myself, I bought a black Labrador puppy called Lucy. I had always wanted a dog of my own, but I hadn't thought it through, and the experience was a nightmare.

The puppy was the result of an unplanned liaison between two Labradors that happened to live next door to each other. I foolishly bought this appealing little animal for ten quid and took her home in a shoe box. I had some sort of vague image of me with the perfectly trained adult dog, basking in its devotion and fondly watching it obey my every calm command. I don't know how I thought I was going to get there.

Of course the little creature was lonely and wailed bitterly all night. In desperation I took her upstairs with me and hung an arm out of bed to fondle her ears every time she cried. Of course she peed everywhere and fouled the floor. It was hideous, and I was too obstinate to admit that I'd made a dreadful mistake. As I now had a new job of wandering poet, I had to go away quite a lot. Bored and baffled, she dragged the stuffing out of my new sofa in my new home. She gnawed the legs of my new table. When I took her out she pulled against the lead with extraordinary strength. It was exhausting; she walked the whole distance on her two back legs. I was at my wits' end.

My dad, Stan, had watched this debacle quietly as it unfolded. He knew how to treat a puppy and, eventually, white with relief, I took her over to my parents' home to live. They took the awful responsibility off my shoulders and gave her a good home. I had made every single mistake in the book and should never have gone within a hundred miles of a dog at that time. I had made no preparations, done no research and had not a clue what to expect. I did at least get this little verse from the harrowing experience, but reading it suggests a lot more light-heartedness than I felt at the time. When I next took on a dog I made sure the circumstances were better, and that I had a serious amount of time to spend on getting both of us off to a good start.

## Puppy Problems

I bought myself a puppy
And I hoped in time he might
Become my friend and ward off
Things that go bump in the night
So I put him in a shoe box
And at home I took him out
And then began to learn
What owning puppies is about.

I tried so hard to love him
And I didn't rave or shout
As he bit into the sofa
And he dragged the stuffing out
I *gave* him things to chew
But soon I couldn't fail to see
That he liked the things he *found*
More than the things supplied by me.

He frayed my lovely carpet
That I'd saved my pennies for
And when he wasn't chewing
He was weeing on the floor,
Nor did he spare the table leg
That came in for a gnaw
Though I told him off the message
Never seemed to reach his jaw.

We laboured at the gardening,
Me and my little pup
At two I planted flowers
And at four he dug them up

He liked to dig, he'd bury bones
And pat it down so neat
And then he'd rush indoors
As clods of mud flew off his feet.

I bought a book on training
And I read it all one night
And when we set off out
I really thought we'd got it right
With titbits in my coat
To give him once he got the knack
But he didn't so I couldn't
So *I* ate them coming back.

When I commanded 'Heel!'
He never seemed to take the point
But galloped on half-strangled
Tugging my arm out of joint
He jumped up people's clothes,
The cleaning bills I had to pay!
And when I shouted 'Here!'
He turned and ran the other way.

One day I drove him over
And I gave him to my dad
Who welcomed him and trained him
But it left me very sad
So I thought I'd let you know
In case a pup's in store for you
That it's very wise indeed
To have a dad who likes dogs too.

## A Slight Howsyourfather

It's a bit … like that … at the moment,
A bit … better left well alone,
A bit … least said soonest mended,
You know … when we're next on our own.

Well, we have had a slight howsyourfather,
A touch of the old you-know-who,
Well, I found her here with him on Friday,
And we did. We had quite a to-do.

It's not that I blame him entirely,
It's not what some people might think,
And he has had his confidence shattered,
Since the whatsisname went on the blink.

I mean it was always a bit of a job,
It was never a hundred per cent,
He had several attacks of the doings,
And the last time it just sort of … went.

I told him: 'Don't bother about it!
Just put it right out of your head!'
But he worried you see and he fretted,
Scratched it of course and it spread.

But it's *her* that I feel took advantage,
She's not like him, she knows the score,

She's always been fond of the need-I-say-what,
With you-know-who, need I say more?

So we're both, as it were, treading lightly,
And nobody's got much to say,
We're all right, more or less, but I have to confess,
That it *is* a bit ... like that ... today.


## Paul O'Chatberg Grogan

He was Paul O'Chatberg Grogan,
He was manly, he was lean,
The sun had bleached his hair
And it was thick and it was clean,
His eyes were cold as chisels,
Far too blue for any man,
And when he gazed on women
Well, they clutched their drawers and ran.

He was Paul O'Chatberg Grogan
Of the long athletic stride,
With long athletic arms
All down his long athletic side,
With long athletic legs;
And those that knew the family well
Said he had a long athletic
History as well.

He was Paul O'Chatberg Grogan,
He could ride and he could hunt,
And when he was at Cambridge
He was mustard with a punt.
He could speak in any language
The world had ever known,
And when he got fed up with that
He wrote one of his own.

He was a demon on the squash court,
And a tyrant in the gym;
He had a spotted belt in judo
(They'd invented it for him).
And when he hit a cricket ball
The sound was like no other's,
For the bat disintegrated
And he had to use his brother's.

Oh his gaze was always level,
His chin was always square,
His voice was always even
And his teeth were always ... there.
He drove a Maserati,
The fastest he could find
And a little string of broken hearts
All flopped along behind.

A Countess shared his life –
From Spain, with eyes as black as coals.
They jetted round the world
With him relaxed at the controls.

And she had hair like ebony,
And she had skin like gold
With hands that felt like butterflies
And feet that felt the cold.

And she had feather pillows
And she had satin sheets,
And Paul O'Chatberg Grogan
Could perform amazing feats.
The feats he could perform,
Cannot be decently revealed,
But a chicken house collapsed,
A mile away out in a field.

Here lies Paul O'Chatberg Grogan,
He is never coming back,
His reflection was so gorgeous
That he had a heart attack.
The lonely Maserati
Is silent on the grass,
And broken hearts jump up
And dash themselves against the glass.

## *Clive the Fearless Birdman*

Clive the fearless birdman was convinced that he could fly,
At night he lay in bed and dreamed of soaring through the sky
Of winging through the clouds, of gliding far out into space
And he had a leather helmet with a beak stuck on the face.

Clive the fearless birdman had a wife who did not care,
For his fly by night ambition of cavorting through the air,
With mockery and ridicule she did her best to kill it,
And cruelly filled his breakfast plate with cuttlefish and millet.

But in his little potting shed he'd built some mighty wings,
Out of balsa wood and sticky tape and plasticine and strings,
Up to his neck in feathers which had taken months to pluck
He laboured with his Evo-Stick, he fashioned and he stuck.

He tried it on at last and slowly turned from side to side
So wonderful was it that Clive the birdman slumped and
    cried,
So shiny were the feathers all in silver grey and black,
With eiderdown all up the front and turkey down the back.

It strapped on with a harness buckled round his arms and
    throat,
All made adjustable to fit the thickness of his coat,
Just to see him walking down the street made women shriek
As he flapped by in his harness and his helmet and his beak.

So Clive announced to all the culmination of his search
And told the local papers he'd be jumping off the church
Seth, the old gravedigger, with his face as black as coal
Said 'If he jumps off the steeple I shan't have to dig a hole.'

And so the day arrived and all the people came to stare
Police held back the crowds and all the local press were there
Clive read out a noble speech, an address to the people
That nobody could hear for it was windy up the steeple.

He stepped out into space and flapped his wings just for a
    minute,
Far above the vicar's garden as he plummeted straight in it
He lay there in the cabbages without another flutter
And the beak came off his helmet and went rolling in the
    gutter.

But far away in Heaven Clive the birdman reigns supreme
Soaring through the air without the aid of jet or steam
So at the Pearly Gates if it's with Clive you wish to speak
You can tell him by his harness and his helmet and his beak.

## The Gardening Man

Oh let us salute him, the gardening man,
Alone with his thoughts and his watering can,
A song in his heart and a pain in his back,
And all his tomatoes are starting to crack.

The fly's on the carrot, the spot's on the rose,
Every joy of the garden he knows,
The feel of the compost, the clink of the pot,
The neck of his onions all starting to rot.

Oh let us admire him, the gardening fellow,
There in his orchard so misty and mellow,
All of its riches he reaches to grab,
And all of his apples are covered in scab.

The thrip's in the privet, the moth's in the peas,
There's fire in his tulips and fire in his knees,
But he tackles them all with a toss of his head,
And a swig of the tackle he keeps in the shed.

The gardener's visage, untroubled and clear,
The wind's in his face and the frost's in his ear,
And though disappointment his hopes may have slain,
Like dust on the Perlite, he rises again.

Disasters too dreadful for dwelling upon,
The night that the heater was never switched on,
When he slept in his bed and he never arose,
While all of his blue cinerarias froze.

But there's always a lawnmower blade to adjust,
Always a hollyhock covered in rust,
The sun's in the heavens, the dew's on the fern,
And the frost on the patio fractured his urn.

A blow for the gardening man let us strike!
The soil's in his blood, bone, and fish if you like,
May his joy never cease as he plants up his trough,
Nor the seedlings of happiness ever ... damp off.

## When I Get up from My Chair

Quiet please! Kindly don't impede my concentration,
I am sitting in the garden thinking thoughts of propagation,
Of sowing and of nurturing, the fruits my work will bear,
And the place won't know what hit it ...

> Once I get up from my chair.

I'm at the planning stages now, if you should need to ask,
And if I'm looking weary, it's the rigours of the task,
Creation of a garden is a strain, as you can guess,
So if my eyes should close, it isn't sleep of course ...

> It's stress.

Oh the leeks that I will dibble and the beans that I will stick,
The bugs that I will slaughter and the seedlings I will prick,
I'll disinfect the greenhouse, I will organise the shed,
And beside my faded roses I will snip off every head.

The mower I will cherish and the tools that I will oil,
The dark nutritious compost I will stroke into the soil,
My sacrifice, devotion and heroic aftercare,
Will leave you green with envy ...
                         Once I get up from my chair.

Oh the weeds that I shall mutilate, the clumps that I will split,
I'm foaming at the mouth just at the very thought of it,
I am heaving at the traces, I am tearing out my hair,
And you'll see a ruddy hero ...
                         Once I get up from my chair.

I will massacre the bindweed and the moss upon the lawn,
That hairy bittercress will curse the day that it was born,
I will rise against the foe and in the fight we will be matched,
And the woolly caterpillars they will curse the day they hatched.

Oh the branches I will layer and the cuttings I will take,
Let other fellows dig a pond – I shall dig a lake,
My garden, what a showpiece! There'll be pilgrims come to stare,
And I'll bow, and take the credit ...
                         Once I get up from my chair.

## Behold My Bold Provider

Behold my bold provider, he can hunt and he can trap,
He can make a set of hinges from a piece of leather strap,
See his trousers fashioned from the finest rabbit skins,
As he sits astride the sawing horse and sews his moccasins.

He can craft a drystone wall and he can build in daub and
  wattle,
There is no cringing rabbit my provider cannot throttle,
His mighty hands in tandem can be simmering the jam,
Making rope soled sandals and delivering a lamb.

Happiness he claims is just a mug of herbal tea,
His own methane digester to provide the energy,
He spurns the wimpish jersey on the Marks & Spencer shelf,
His is brown and knobbly, he knitted it himself.

He stalks the dripping undergrowth and coppices the ash,
And pities the commuters in their early morning dash,
Till, weary from his labours he may pause from splitting logs,
To rest and gnaw a bone and fling the gristle to the dogs.

We're having goat tonight although the meat is very tough,
He's made the goatsmilk cheese. I only wish I liked the stuff,
Here he comes with nature's riches all for me to pluck,
Twenty-seven partridges, a gander and a duck.

Wearing all these skins he cured himself to keep him warm,
I see him at the beehive as he juggles with a swarm,

Or in the glowing lamplight all is harmony and peace,
As we sit before the open fire and card another fleece.

Our dinner's in the haybox and my frock is on the loom,
My provider's gone aloft to thatch another room,
And I give thanks eternal that of all the roles in life,
Mine, by great good fortune, was a bold provider's wife.


# A Card Through Your Door

I was asked to speak at a conference of greetings card manufact-
urers. The following four verses were some of my (none-too-serious)
suggestions.


## *Good Luck in Your Exam*

Against your every answer
May the teacher place a tick,
And if by chance he doesn't,
Well, you can't help being thick!


## *Get Well Soon*

I hope you have recovered
And your legs are out of plaster
Your wife's moved in with me
So don't get better any faster!

## *On Your Wedding*

Good luck on your wedding day,
I think you're bold and plucky,
And as the other two have failed,
Let's hope it's third time lucky!

## *As You Retire*

Now can you release the weary tiller
The ship of life, with you upon the prow,
Is heaving to at last in calmer waters,
In other words you're on the scrap heap now.

## *Pat-a-cake*

Pat-a-cake, Pat-a-cake
Baker's man
Bake us a cake
As fast as you can
But wash your hands
Before you invite us
'Cause we don't want
Gastro-enteritis!

## The Harvest Hymn

All is safely gathered in, the barns are filled with grain,
Now our thoughts of summer turn to winter once again,
The animals of Eden two by two came in the Ark,
So can I have a husband now the nights are getting dark?

I do not want a handsome man all other girls would crave,
One like Auntie Ann's who sent her to an early grave,
He took all of her money and whatever else he could grab,
She went all round the orchard but she finished up with a crab.

In all the mighty multitudes upon the land and sea,
Have you got a surplus man who might just do for me?
A big one or a small one, white as snow or black as soot,
And preferably one to wait upon me hand and foot.

We thank thee for the ears of corn that springeth from the sod
And from the paths of righteousness O never have I trod
There was the one occasion when I had that gin and lime
and things got out of hand but still I stopped him just in time.

I laid aside temptation and I turned the other cheek,
The spirit it is willing but the flesh is getting weak,
I raise my voice beseechingly and ask with one accord,
O please send me a man who looks a bit like Harrison Ford.

*I wrote this song to be sung to the tune of 'The Ballad of Jimmy Brown' also known as 'Three Bells'.*

## The Insects' Anthem

We. We the assembled.
Do hereby pledge a solemn vow,
If any of us be faint-hearted,
Let him leave the party now.
Our comrades all have gone to glory,
We will not see their like again,
They figured briefly in life's story,
And now are numbered with the slain.

We are gathered here together,
Recalling creatures great and small,
Their names are on the roll of honour,
Here upon the garden wall,

These are the heroes of our nation,
These are the victims of the spray,
All those who fell in rotovation,
And all forms of cultivation,
We remember them today.

Friends. Friends and neighbours,
And all dependants of the soil,
We, whose lives are overshadowed,
In every aspect of our toil,
For those who cling to vegetation,
Inhabitants of bean and pea,
Those who wade upon the water
And those in peril ... up a tree.

We see them bearing down upon us,
Armed with their implements and hoes,
We see them marching down the furrows,
To give us all a bloody nose,

We live in fear of persecution,
Our song of freedom must be sung,
And those of us they have beheaded,
Pruned and composted and shredded,
Lie abandoned in the dung.

So, in condemnation
Of evil deeds and slaughter foul
Those, so murderously taken,
By the dibble and the trowel
For those that tremble in the darkness
For those whose roots are far below,
Who dread, the whistle of the strimmer,
And the man, who went to mow.

Weevils mites and hairy spiders,
Aphids ladybirds and bees
Gather round in supplication,
On their bended hairy knees
From the bondage of oppression
We will one day all be free
Every creepy every crawly,
Every martyr gone to glory
In the name of liberty
(*heroic big finish:*)
*Liberty, Li-ber-TEEEEEEEE!

*A flag may be waved at this dramatic moment.*

## The Exiled Gum

Don't water me no more my friend,
Don't water me no more.
I am an exiled Eucalypt
Far from my native shore.
If I'd have been in Sydney
I might have made a show,
But I've been sent to England
And I ain't going to grow.

Don't stand me on the window sill
And pluck out every weed,
Don't sprinkle me with potash
To germinate me seed.
Me little heart is broken
My country was my all
If I can't sprout where the kookaburras shout
Well, I don't want to sprout at all.

I'll never feel the rolling paddy melons
Bump me trunk,
I'll never probe the stubbies there
And get a little drunk.
Not for me the Tasman Sea
To watch the breakers roll
For I am in the window
In a tasteful copper bowl.

And a gum tree's heart's so fearless
He must face the searing drought,
But in this English sitting room

There's not much drought about.
And of the raging bushfires
I do not see a lot
Except for when her husband
Stubs his fag out in me pot.

I need Australian sunshine,
I need the blistering heat,
A wedgetailed eagle on me head
And a wombat at me feet.
I want to grow where Mother stood
I want to be there too.
Oh Mother dear, where are you now?
Gone for a canoe.

Farewell you noble eucalypts
Our roots shall ne'er entwine
Underneath Australia,
For they have potted mine.
Me little shoot has wilted
But it's facing to the east
Good sailing, dearest Mother
From the exiled gum, deceased.

## Lost in Transit

I left my heart in Australia
I left my knees in Japan
I left my liver
Up the Yangtze River
And I'm only half a man.

## *Jim*

Dear Jim, We've had your letter and your dad's deciphered that,
As I fried him up some sausages in deep nutritious fat,
I think of you out there while we're awake and you're asleep,
And I think of you each Friday when you used to pay your keep.

Your letter is a treasure, made us cry and made us laugh,
Thank you for the kisses in the final paragraph,
We loved the surfing photo, laughing, hands upon your hips,
And Dad says what's that white stuff you've got plastered
    round your lips?

My son, you know your leaving was a sore distress to me,
So your dad kindly took me out to *Crocodile Dundee*,
Therefore I am sending separately in a box,
My bone-handled breadknife should you need to stab the crocs.

We found it quite a trial when we had seen you board the
    plane,
Climbing in the car and driving homeward once again,
Those magazines beneath your bed, Dad took away to store,
He found them very interesting and can he have some more?

My son I feel your presence though you're far across the seas,
I seem to hear your name 'Jim' as a whisper on the breeze,
I'm grieving for you sweetheart, no son gave his mother more,
I can't bring myself to touch your underclothes dropped on the
    floor.

Indeed your aching absence is tormenting Dad and me,
So we have hatched a little plot as you will shortly see,
We've counted up our savings and we know it's not too late,
Jim! We have decided that *we're* going to emigrate!

We've filled in all the papers and your dad has had the jabs,
He's handed in his notice and the house is up for grabs,
So clear a little corner of your condominium,
We'll be there a week on Monday, lots of love from Dad
    and Mum!


## No Alarm on the Flight Deck

I wrote this after I read a report that an airline pilot, with his
aircraft on automatic pilot, had fallen asleep at the controls and
had to be woken by members of the crew!

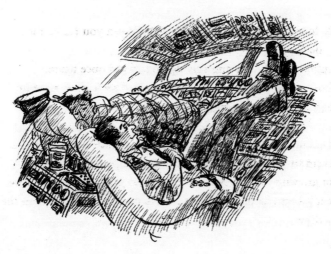

## No Alarm on the Flight Deck

We're on automatic pilot and the lights are soft and low,
The passengers are sleeping wrapped in blankets, row on row,
But I'm on full alert on every aeroplane I take,
One question always haunts me: 'Is the pilot still *awake*?'

Up beyond the curtain is he slumped at the controls,
Sleeping like a baby with an aircraft full of souls,
Are we in his Jumbo, DC-10 or one eleven
On a one way ticket not to Sydney but to Heaven?

Has he got a little bedside table for his cash,
Does he put his slippers on and cross them on the dash,
As the automatic pilot steers us out across the deep,
Does he slacken off his tie and gently fall asleep?

Droning through the cumulus, dancing with the dawn,
Does the pilot shift a little, stretch himself and yawn,
As the sun appears, flirtatious, pink upon the brow,
Does he idly wonder 'Where the blazes are we now?'

Does he struggle upright, shrugging on his pilot's coat,
And chipper to the crew say 'Well, the old bus stayed afloat!'
As the panorama is unfurling underneath,
Is he lifting up the glass and fishing out his teeth?

As a ray of sun illuminates the line of dials,
Does he rub his eyes and say 'Good grief! We've done some
    miles!'

Seeing his co-pilot does he gently pat his hand,
And softly say 'Wake up! I think we're coming in to land!'

Bronzed and manly pilot, here's a message from the rear,
Do not fall asleep for we're all counting on you here,
Keep your wits about you as you circle, as you climb,
So we can die of fright when coming back in six weeks' time.

## Ayers Rock

Daybreak over Ayers Rock –
The Centre's breath was bated.
Snakes slid down their tunnels
And a huntsman spider waited.
Little grieving redbacks wandered,
Never could they rest:
Searching, ever searching
For the seat they loved the best.

But an enigmatic figure
Stood beside the Uluru,
With one lip curled in scorn
The way the real explorers do.
The day was growing hotter
But she calmly scanned the skies,
Covered up with 'Aeroguard'
And half-a-million flies.

She wore her expedition clothes –
She'd planned this day for months:
The shorts that Burke and Wills
Could both have travelled in at once,
The tennis shoes Bjorn Borg
Had signed along the side –
Behold! Pam Ayres the mountaineer!
Oh! Speak her name with pride!

I set out from the Uluru
All in my digger's hat,
And forty others set out
But we won't go into that.
I scaled the mighty mountainside
And folks we chanced to meet
Cried out, 'Here comes Pam Ayres!
She must have suckers on her feet!'

I was frank and I was fearless,
I threw away my coat
And, lunging for the summit,
I was like a mountain goat,
A party from Whyalla
Was clinging to the chain
And hollered down the line,
'She's overtaking us … again!'

But the vista from the summit
Was a marvel to behold.
I signed the special book
Although my hands were stiff with cold.

The mighty Olgas slumbered on
So beautiful and round
As though a giant horse had paused
To fertilise the ground.

Yet as I stood surveying
This extraordinary place,
I thought I felt a drop of rain
Roughly smite me face.
The skies began to open,
My heart began to sink
And in five minutes time
Ayers Rock was like a skating rink.

The Bjorn Borgs were sodden
They'd cost me oh so dear!
He might have helped on the Centre Court
But he couldn't help me here.
I couldn't get a purchase!
I couldn't get a grip!
And everywhere I placed me feet
Me feet began to slip!

There was nothing to hold on to!
I quickly gave up hope.
In my imagination
I fell screaming down the slope.
I heard me mother weeping
As she clutched my digger's hat,
I heard the poets of the world
Say, 'Thank the Lord for that!'

I said to my companion,
'Will you see I get a plaque?
Not the dental kind
The one for not arriving back.
Fix it high above the road,
Write "Poet of Renown:
Pam Ayres the Ayers Rock heroine
Who slipped up coming down".'

But no, I did not falter,
Though my shoes had lost their soles,
Though the shorts that Burke and Wills
Could both have worn were shot with holes,
But if I hadn't made it
And downward had been hurled
At least I would have had
The biggest headstone in the world!

## Hello Australia, Hello!

Oh, it's nice to be back in Australia –
I wanted to see it again.
I came on the Sydney Tomorrow Bird
Though I'd half expected a 'plane.
As we came sweeping over the harbour
The sunset was close on our heels
Over Mountains Blue, Woolloomooloo,
And Harry's Café de Wheels.

Oh, it's nice to be back in Australia,
The land of the Desert Pea –
If it's good enough for Edna
Then it's good enough for me.
It's the land of Banjo Paterson,
The shearing shed, the flock –
He's the man from Snowy River
I'm the woman from Ayers Rock.

Oh, pass me that Pavlova
All drenched in kiwi fruit,
And drive me out in the mulga
With a roo bar on the ute,
And underneath a stringybark
I'll see what passes through –
A currawong might fly along
And the odd thorn-bird or two.

Oh, the Lamingtons bloom in Sydney
And food no one can resist
Which might be why each man goes by
With a meat pie in his fist.
I'm glad to be back in Australia
And it'll be beaut I know
If I see you about, I'll pick up the shout,
Hello Australia, Hello!

# Hello Long Distance, Is That You?

It's hard to realise now what a tremendous event a long-distance telephone call used to be. People booked them up for Christmas or important family occasions and looked forward to the day when they would hear the longed-for voice of loved ones who had moved far away, often those who had emigrated to Australia or New Zealand. There was absolutely nothing spontaneous about them. You were given a time slot and if, for whatever reason, your call did not 'come through' then the disappointment was shattering.

To receive the call, actually to converse across the vast oceans, was extraordinary. Each member of the family would anxiously wait their turn to lovingly hold the receiver. The only drawback was, at that distance and after long separations, there were often only a few stock questions that could reasonably be asked. Nevertheless, as each member of the family came tremulously forward to take up the phone, asked they were, over and over and over again ...

## Hello Long Distance, Is That You?

Hello? Hello? Hello? Hello?
Oh, hello, Mum! It's *me*!
Hello! How are you keeping?
Yes, I can. Can you hear me?
How is everybody? Alright?
Yes and we are too.
It's twenty-five past seven here –
What time is it with you?

Ay? Dad would like a word?
Oh, he's just coming on, I see.
Hello! How are you, Dad?
Oh yes I *can*. Can you hear me?
How is everybody? Alright?
Yes, and we are too.
Twenty-five past seven, Dad,
What time is it with you?

Well, Dad, how's the weather?
How's the weather, nice I s'pose?
I said how-is-the-weather?
How's the WEATHER? (Stone the crows!)
Dad? Just call to Mum,
I think she's on the bedroom phone.
I can't hear you *both*
Tell her to leave that one alone.

Ay? Who asked me that?
Was that you, Dad? Oh, it was Mum.
Twenty-five past seven here –
Rain? We have had some,
It rained up to the Wednesday
'Cause I had the ear-ache
And then it brightened up ...
No! It was Thursday (my mistake).

We had this thunderstorm:
It scared us all out of our wits.
Oh, it upset Mrs White –
That Mrs White who has the fits ... no, FITS!
Hello? I thought I'd lost you –
No, I'd got the dialling tone.
Try not to shout so loud, Dad,
Dad? Why don't you use the phone?

All right then, better go then
Or we shan't afford the bill.
Just *gone* half past seven, Dad,
So long then ... Yes we will,
All the best, mind how you go
And Dad? Stay off the booze!
Enjoy the rain, I'll ring again
*Next* time I've got some news.

## How God Made the Duck-Billed Platypus

I first toured Australia in 1978 and have been back regularly ever since. It's a great privilege to work in a different country, alongside real people, and not have to go as a tourist being chaperoned round the sights by someone with a flag and an itinerary. For economic reasons, though, tour dates are fairly closely packed together, and it's frustrating to have to hurry past interesting places you would have loved to investigate. Days off are precious and busy.

I was playing a theatre in Melbourne during my first tour when we had a day off, and friends took us to visit the Healesville Sanctuary, a type of zoo. Here I saw my first duck-billed platypus. Then it was housed in a rather miserable, coffin-shaped tank made of thick glass. It probably has nicer accommodation now; I hope so. Anyway, I watched the platypus undulate up and down, and it seemed to me to be such an odd combination of ingredients: webbed feet, beak, fur, eggs, babies – everything had been thrown in. I thought perhaps God had made him from all the pieces he had left over when he'd finished making everybody else.

## How God Made the Duck-Billed Platypus

The duck-billed platypus, small aquatic friend
Made from the pieces God had over at the end.
According to His reckoning (He'd not been wrong before)
He hadn't made enough: He needed one mammal more.

He studied all the corners in his cupboard large and bare
A little foot here, and a little nose there,
A scrap of fur, a feather, nothing anyone would miss
And God said, 'Oh Good God … Yes? … What can I make
   out of this?'

There was a funny flat tail and a great enormous beak
Which had lain in the cupboard for a year and a week,
There were four webbed feet in the manner of a duck
And hanging on a peg a furry overcoat for luck!

So the turn of the platypus came to be fitted
God sat him down and he honestly admitted
That the finished platypus might appear a little odd,
'But look on the bright side of it,' said God.

'You can swim in the river, you can paddle in the creek,
You can tackle *anybody* with a great big beak,

There's a tail for a rudder or alternatively legs
And by way of consolation you've got babies *and* eggs.'

So God took all the pieces into Workshop One
And there he told the men the sort of thing he wanted done.
The Carpenter and Plumber stroked the platypus's neck
And said, 'Don't you upset him, he can't run but he can peck!'

So the platypus was made, and his beak was firmly rooted,
And God found him a home where he would not be persecuted.
They packed him up and sent him with his tail neatly furled
In a brown paper parcel marked 'Australia, The World'.

## The Slimming Poem

I'm a slimmer by trade, I'm frequently weighed,
I'm slim as a reed in the river.
I'm slender and lean, and hungry and mean –
Have some water, it's good for your liver.

Don't give me cheese rolls or profiteroles,
Don't show me that jelly a-shakin',
Don't give me cream crackers, picnickers and snackers
Or great big ice-creams with a flake in.

Don't give me swiss roll or toad-in-the-hole,
Don't show me that Black Forest gateau.
You sit and go mouldy you old garibaldi
Your pastry all riddled with fat. Oh!

When fat I feel weary and tubby and dreary
The stairs make me struggle and grunt dear,
And yet I'm so happy and punchy and snappy.
With hip bones all stuck out the front dear.

No, it's white fish for me, no milk in me tea
And if we don't like it we lump it,
No figs or sultanas, no mashed-up bananas,
No pleasure and no buttered crumpet.

Don't get any bigger, me old pear-shaped figure
I can and I will become thinner.
So cheer up and take heart, pass the calorie chart,
Let's see what we're having for dinner!

## Aerobics

Well, Mother, did I make a fool of myself,
Last night on the bathroom floor,
I'm so out of shape so I put on the tape
That I sent to the TV for,
Well on came the voice of the expert,
With advice to be careful and slow,
But I thought I knew best, I flung off me vest,
And I thought 'Right-O Mother, let's go!'

I bought my John McEnroe trainers,
My how expensive they've grown,
But the thing with this pair, is if I'm not there,
They can run round the block on their own,

I did buy my husband some Reeboks,
I'm afraid they're too high-tech for me,
You pump up the slack, flames shoot out the back,
And you slow down this side of Dundee.

Then I did bicycling exercises,
By Golly, I gave it what for,
Flat on me back with me knees going 'crack'
As the draught whistled under the door,
I borrowed your leotard, Mother,
The one that enhances me charms,
Thanks very much but it went at the crutch
When I started rotating me arms.

I bought my dear husband a tracksuit,
He said terry towelling is best,
With a curl of his lip, he did up the zip,
And took all the hair off his chest,
*And* I bought him an exercise cycle,
The price would have made a man wince,
He never got *off* for a fortnight,
And he's never been *on* the thing since!

We thought we might go on a fun run,
We went with a very nice friend,
He'd not run before and he won't any more,
No, they stretchered him off in the end.
I have had a dabble at tennis,
I jog now and then and I swim,
And I've just met this yoga instructor …
I'm off for a dabble with him!

# Building Sites Bite!

In 1978 the Health and Safety Executive launched a campaign aimed at reducing the number of injuries sustained by children playing on building sites. I was sent an horrific list of accidents and was asked to contribute something in verse form to the campaign.

## *Building Sites Bite!*

This is a horror story
And it's worse because it's true.
Dan Sandheap and Fred the Hole
Have come to talk to you,
Claude the concrete mixer,
Mick the Brick and Cable Man
Have come here from a building site
To warn you if they can.

Claude the concrete mixer
Came up shuffling to the front.
He said, 'All day on building sites
It's back and forth I shunt.
The workmen prop me up
And rush away to eat their lunch,
So you play under me
So I can fall upon you ... CRUNCH!'

Fred the Hole spoke up,
His voice as deep as any grave,
'Climb in me one rainy day
And down the walls will cave!

172

I'll trap you in the bottom
Where no one can hear you shout
Or see you in the mud and muck
Nor run to get you out.'

Dan the sandheap piped up with,
'They think they're at the sea
When they spy my lovely sand,
They run and climb on me
And then I tumble down on them,
All slippery and seething.
I cover them in sand and soon
I can't feel any breathing ... '

For building sites are dangerous –
Great lorries rush about
And just one lick from Mick the Brick
Is sure to knock you out.
Cable Man said, 'I'm just one
Bare wire here alone
But touch me with your fingers
And I'll burn you skin and bone.'

On building sites these horrid creatures live
And many more,
So please don't *play* on building sites
It's not what they are for.
They're full of danger everywhere
Scattered all about.
Too many children venture in
And never come back out.

# Heaps of Stuff

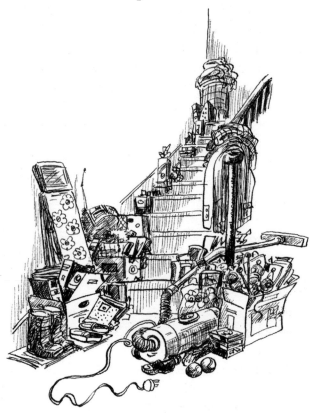

One of my four brothers has a great expression, 'Pleased to see you cupboards'. This is where, on opening the doors of a cupboard , the crammed contents are so delighted to see you that they all fall out on your head.

I love a book called *The Secret of How to Win Freedom from Clutter* by Don Aslett as it contains the world's most sensible advice. In a magazine I was reading ages ago, Maeve Binchy nominated it as her life-changing read and, interested, I tracked it down. Don Aslett points out the daftness of hoarding more and more stuff we don't need, of packing our homes with it, of dusting, protecting and insuring it, of finding new shelves, cupboards and, eventually, houses to contain it all. It rang true for me – I am hopeless at parting with mementoes of the past.

These days I try to be more ruthless, but heaps of stuff still haunt me. You can see them slyly starting to form on the kitchen table. The beginnings look very innocent. All it takes is an odd catalogue, that letter that's a chore to answer, the interesting article it seems such a shame to throw away ...

### Heaps of Stuff

How I wish that I was tidy
How I wish that I was neat
How I wish I was methodical
Like others down our street.
I tried to stem the rising tide
I tried to hold it back
But I have been the victim
Of a heap of stuff attack.

Yes, heaps of stuff come creeping,
They clutter up the hall.
And heaps of stuff are softly
Climbing halfway up the wall.
At each end of the staircase
Is a giant heap, a stack;
One to carry up the stairs
And one to carry back.

In a heap of stuff invasion
They settle everywhere –
They grovel on the lino
They tower on the chair.
You're searching for a jacket,
'Is it in here?' you shout,
And, opening the cupboard door,
A heap of stuff falls out.

But heaps are many-faceted
And heaps are multi-faced
And what a heap is made of
Will depend on where it's placed.
Now if it's in the passage
It is mostly boots and shoes
And if it's on the sofa
It is magazines and news.

If it's in the shed
It's broken propagating frames
And if it's in the bathroom
Well, it's best to say no names,
And if it's in the bedroom –
Your own and not the guest's –
The heap of stuff is mostly made
Of socks and shirts and vests.

For a heap is indestructible,
It's something you can't fight.
If you split it up by day
It joins back up at night.

So cunningly positioned
As from room to room you trek,
Increasing all the chances
That you trip and break your neck.

But step into my parlour
Now I've forced the door ajar;
I'll excavate an easy chair –
Just cling there where you are.
And together we'll survey it
Till our eyes they feast enough
On the tidiest home in England
Underneath the heaps of stuff.

## All Dust and Rubble

I have got the builders in –
It's not a lot of trouble;
Choking in the dust
And falling over in the rubble.
But I shall see much clearer
Once my lintels have been raised,
And come the revolution
We shall all be double glazed.

They're hacking at the plaster
And they're tearing up the floor.
Don't go out! The painter's
Slapping primer on the door.

My little dog gets in the way
They say, 'Come out me dear!'
If I'm in the room –
If not, they kick her in the rear.

I'm the only one who doesn't have
A job to do.
Everybody's sprinting past
With chunks of four by two.
I make the tea at ten
And then I make some more at three,
And while I'm on the subject
Would *you* like a cup of tea?

The plumber's very nice
Although his hair is white with dust.
Chase me if you like
But chase the pipework if you must.
Every window's open
The wind is like a knife
And the Sparks is cracking
Pornographic jokes about his wife.

They switched off the electric,
They didn't tell me why.
The central heating boiler's
Stiff and cold and so am I.
But I mustn't be downhearted!
I'll wash up and make a drink!
But there isn't any water
And there isn't any sink.

Oh, wrap me in a dustsheet
Till my wood has all been sealed,
Till my tiles have all been grouted
And my stonework all revealed.
Eradicate my infestations!
Fill my cavities with foam!
Normal life will be resumed
When the builders have gone home.

## Bournemouth

He was long and tall and thin and dull
And so was she,
He dried his trim moustache
When they had drunk their China tea.
And he was very quiet, very rich
And rather kind,
With one eye that could see
And with the other, which was blind.

His hair was rather sandy
And his manner rather terse,
His clothes were very dull and safe
But then, well, so were hers.
Her shoes were very dear
And never purchased on a whim,
They toned in with the wardrobe
And it was the same with him.

She couldn't really claim,
That as he read the *Business News*
And regaled her now and then
With his opinions and views,
That his figure was endearing
In the fat expensive chair,
Flecked about with dandruff
From his thin and sandy hair.

And neither in his heart
Could he blossom and rejoice
To listen to her speaking
In her flat and toneless voice,
To watch her rosebud mouth
Which would habitually melt
Into a little smile
She always smiled but never felt.

But they got along together
And they liked the same shampoo,
And he was so polite
With 'Oh dear lady: After you!'
And when they walked on Sunday
He would always take her hand
And hold it like a cold dead fish
Washed up along the strand.

Most weekends you could see him
Striding out across the links
While she would be presiding
By the double drainer sinks,
Their meals were full of elegance

But never full of mirth,
Rosé and white and lobster bright
And foods that cost the earth.

And as she whipped the cream
And folded in a little more,
She saw the dark-eyed sailors
As they lingered on the shore.
And he sat on the verandah
With his *Telegraph* and *Punch*
And watched the young girls laughing
As he waited for his lunch.

## Ned Sails in the Sunset

Don't play me them nostalgic ballads, Eunice,
You know it breaks my aching heart in two,
You know it makes me think of darlin' Neddy
And how such men are far between ... and few.
I still can see him standing on the quayside,
In his uniform and all, he looked so grand
With gold braid gleaming all around his helmet
And a Cornish pastie steaming in his hand.

'Goodbye my love!' he cried, his throat constricted,
'You are my comfort and my sustenance!'
He faltered and I thought emotion choked him
But he'd tried to eat the pastie all at once.
I held him and beseeched him, 'Sail in safety!
Journey through the darkness to the light!
May Providence protect your tattered rigging
And hold your rudder steady in the night!'

He turned to board the craft, my heart was aching,
Crying, 'Ned ... shall I never see you more?'
But he brushed away the salt spray from his eyebrow
And resolutely shut the cabin door.
I watched his boat sail off into the sunset,
A thousand violins began to play,
And I thought I saw an old tomato sandwich
Tossing back and forth among the spray.

A mile off shore the fog came down to shroud him,
It hid the Channel Ferry from his view,
It sliced his boat in half, the back and front end
And Ned was standing in between the two.
They sent the air-sea rescue out to find him
But just a Cornish pastie stayed afloat.
Don't play me them nostalgic ballads, Eunice
For Ned and I are severed ... like his boat.

## The Beach Lovers

Come and walk beside me
For the sun is sinking low
And together to the edges
Of the ocean we shall go,
And all our rosy future
In perspective we shall put
Stepping lightly on the rubbish
As it moulders underfoot.
Where all the plastic bottles
Blow across the golden sand
And old refrigerators
Know the tide's caressing hand,
We'll breathe the sweet aroma,
I will take your hand for ever,
Across life's broken glass,
And I shall jettison you never.

*I wrote this for a TV programme on adult literacy. It's about those maddening times when you just can't think of the right word.*

## *Nice*

You see, I've always liked him and last night he took me out,
I'm just a normal girl you see but him, he's been about,
He took me to the pictures and it didn't half cost a price,
So I want to write and tell him that I found it really ... nice.

Oh he took me to the pictures, it was brilliant and then,
Well you see the point is this, well I should like to go again,
So I thought I'd write a note, Oh can *you* give me some advice,
To try and get it over that I think he's really ... nice.

I don't want to look too forward, I don't want to look too fast,
I don't want the first time out with him to also be the last,
He took me for a Chinese meal, for crispy duck with rice,
And we had banana fritters. Oh it *was*, Oh it was ... nice.

He took me home that evening, it was dark and it was late,
When I got in I really felt I'd like to celebrate,
He was all I hankered for, the time had vanished in a trice,
And I couldn't get to sleep because it all had been so ... nice.

I just want to write and *thank* him but I don't know what to say,
I can't put what I feel, it all comes out a different way,
Well it's *stupid*, what I've written, this is why I need advice,
It says: 'Thanks for Friday evening, I enjoyed it. It was ... nice.'

## *The Old Gloucester Sausage*

Of all the counties and the shires so varied and so wide,
Each one has some local dish they speak about with pride,
Roly poly pudding, Bara brith or Bacon Clanger,
But those in Gloucestershire need only mention their own banger.
It's the old Gloucester sausage, that'll make you smack your chops,
And in its manufacture they have pulled out all the stops,
A great majestic sausage with a great majestic name,
And beside it any other sausage hangs its head with shame.

Oh, the old Gloucester sausage, that's a meal for any man,
You can tell the way it sits up proud and noble in the pan,
You can keep your Cornish pastie, you can have your sausage roll,
But an old Gloucester sausage with its skin as black as coal,
Well! Can anyone imagine any nicer sight than that?
To stab it with your pocket knife and see that squirt of fat,
To drop it in the frying pan, to push it to the front,
And on a winter's morning you can hear the beggar grunt.

Oh the old Gloucester sausage, that'll give your life a spark,
Granny had a spasm when she grabbed one in the dark,
Grandad he had eaten one the night he said 'Be mine!'
And though his eyes grew dim his whiskers never failed to shine.
The old Gloucester sausage, fully stuffed in every part,
The final great achievement of the sausage stuffer's art,
Bursting at the seams with healthy meat and fat and gristle,
Cereal and rusk and even little tufts of bristle.

Oh the old Gloucester sausage, it's a masterpiece it's true,
You can grill it, you can fry it, you can stick it up the flue,
You can jab it, you can prick it, or for something even rougher,
You can hit it with a frying pan and really make it suffer.
Let the gourmet gabble, only other gourmets listen,
Never on his fork will any Gloucester sausage glisten,
Never will he hear it sizzle, prick it fore and aft,
And stick it down the skirting board to counteract the draught.

Oh the old Gloucester sausage, that'll make the weak the strong,
The old Gloucester sausage, that'll make the short the long,
The old Gloucester sausage that'd melt a heart of stone,
A pound of them and you could plough the parish on your own.
So when your sturdy son sets out upon his daily round,
His mighty hobnails ringing on the cold and frosty ground,
Be contented Missis as you bid your lad good day,
For an old Gloucester sausage is behind him, all the way.

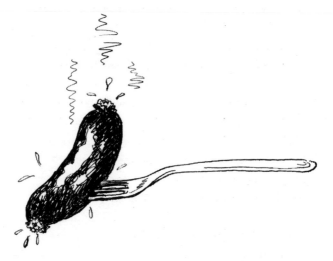

## *Once I Was a Looker and So Was My Spouse*

Once I was a looker and so was my spouse
I recall when we first came to live in this house
He was young, optimistic and fresh in the face
With never the twang of a hernia brace.

He said he would die if he could not be mine
He wooed me with words more addictive than wine
The monastery beckoned, he wanted no other
But now he troops in and he says 'Ulloo Mother.'

He'd bound through the door with a laugh and a slap
And I used to think 'My, there's a handsome young chap
Thank Heavens I'm wed to a red-blooded man'
But now I get pecks like you'd give your old Gran.

He used to take pains with the look of his hair
The top London salons, they all knew him there
No end ever split and no high standard slid
Now he goes round to George who'll oblige for a quid.

But when he first courted me, wasn't I proud
His gay repartee had me laughing out loud
But now he reclines in his jersey and socks
And in my direction grunts 'What's on the box?'

I used to look on as he walked down the street
A picture of style from his head to his feet

But now there's a cap where the tresses have thinned
And faded old trousers that flap in the wind.

Mind I'm not blameless, I know very well
That the strain of maternity's starting to tell
I do what I can but there's one thing for sure
The mirror is no friend of mine any more.

He used to admire my refinement and poise
I'd turn up my nose at a smell or a noise
But now when I'm shouting he ducks with the rest
As I go haring past with a po and a vest.

Oh yes he admired the cut of my jib
And wasn't I thin? You could see every rib
But now in the chrome at the top of the cooker
I see many things, but I can't see a looker.

## Walk with Me for a Perch and a Rood

I don't want metrication, friends,
The milligramme and litre,
I work in feet and inches,
I do not trust the metre.
I cannot calculate it,
I don't know where I am,
Give me half a hundredweight
And you can have a gramme.

Metrication? I can't learn it,
I'm too long in the tooth,
My schooldays they are over,
Gorn! with the bloom of youth.
I work in tenths of inches,
The furlong and the chain,
The rood and pole, the six-foot hole,
I like it nice and plain.

I like it by the furlong,
And I like it by the acre,
I liked the baker's dozen,
And I also liked the baker.
I liked the bushel basket,
And a peck's alright by me,
Them metrics put the prices up
As far as I can see.

I didn't want the decimals,
I don't want metrication,
I wouldn't know a litre
If you poured it in a basin.
I'll have my pints and gallons
As long as I am able,
My glass I'll fill with a sixth of a gill,
And I'll see you under the table!

*Pam Ayres*

*Robbie Burns was apparently a devilishly handsome man. He had
dark shining eyes and women found him extremely attractive.*

## On Comparing My Husband to Robbie Burns

Oh oft I think of Robbie Burns,
Striding through the heather,
All manly clad in tartan plaid
To spurn the Highland weather,
O'er loch and glen, that man of men,
His black eyes all a-flashing
Could any heart not leap, and start,
Or fail to find him dashing?
Oh oft I think of Robbie Burns,
His dirk thrust in his gaiters,
And then I think of you dear,
And go home and peel the taters.

## The Neglected Wife's Valentine

Some men have a wonderful ability to choose gifts for their wife or partner. Regardless of expense or inconvenience to themselves, they can home in on the one specific item that will make their wife or partner feel singled out, important and cherished.

One Valentine's Day my husband bought me a step-ladder. I felt so deflated that anyone could think this was a suitable gift on a romantic occasion like Valentine's Day that my reception of the step-ladder was frosty. In fact it was arctic. Consequently, the next Valentine's Day I received nothing at all. My husband was heard to mutter, 'Serves you right,' as he went chortling off. In my disappointment and indignation I wrote the following short appeal.

### *The Neglected Wife's Valentine*

Won't someone send me a Valentine to make my husband jealous?
Something big and gaudy, altogether over-zealous,
Write upon it 'Pam, my heart stands still when you walk past …'
And when my husband sees it, he might notice me at last.

Oh write me something torrid, like 'I'm burning with desire!
Meet me in Mustique before me underclothes catch fire!'
My husband will be staggered, he will read it like a book,
And think 'Well, *someone* fancies her, I'll have another look!'

Go on, write me something saucy, so my husband will be miffed,
Like 'You won't need your pyjamas, if you kind of … get my drift.'
I'll leave it on the mantelpiece and when he rushes through,
He'll read it and then next year *he* might think to send one too.

*A word to those planning to keep sheep:*

## Fleeced

I bought a flock of sheep because my garden seemed so bare,
I thought they'd eat the grass and add a touch of interest there,
The soil was alkali, oh there were mice and there were ants,
So I thought I'd get some sheep because the frost had my
    chrysanths.

First they ate the grass and then the borders and the shrubs,
The blue and white lobelia, the alpines in the tubs,
I had to get some grazing to accommodate my sheep,
With a shelter and a water trough and none of it came cheap.

Now I love my little flock but I have had to come to terms
With dipping, shearing, dagging, dosing, drenching them for
    worms
And on a winter's afternoon not dozing by the fire,
But trying to free a sheep that's got its head stuck in the wire.

And then they get diseases, they get fluke and they get mange,
They get footrot, they get orf, they might get scrapie for a
    change,
And when it comes to lambing time the nights are cold and black,
With just you, the soapy water and a lamb with both legs back.

Consider very carefully before you buy a sheep,
They need constant supervision and you won't get any sleep,
You'll have to pay the rent, the vet, the drugs, the food, the licks,
And you'll have to be adept at extricating bloated ticks.

If you keep a ram, yes, he'll look noble in the clover,
But when your back is turned he'll do his best to knock you over,
But if without a flock of sheep you'll waste away and pine,
Then come and talk to me as I should like to give you mine!

## The Horse's Farewell to His Cowboy

Farewell to you cowboy, my day it is done,
Of rounding up cows in the heat of the sun,
Of roping the dogies and branding the steer,
And having your gun going off in my ear.
I galloped the prairie without any thanks,
Your great silver spurs in my bony old flanks,
And I've seen many things in my life it is true,
But never a cowboy more stupid than you.

*Chorus:*
Cowboy can you hear me inside the saloon?
I'm waiting out here in the light of the moon,
My hardworking days they are past and gone by,
And I'm bound for the great clover field in the sky.

Farewell to the feel of your filthy old jeans,
Farewell to the smell of your coffee and beans,
Farewell to you in your stetson and chaps,
Cheating at poker and shooting the craps.
You rode me too fast and you rode me too far,
Mile after mile of you shouting 'Yee har!'
Hounded by outlaws away down the track,
With a gun on my tail and a berk on my back.

193

I never remember you treating me right,
I was tied to a cactus and hungry all night,
When I was weary and dying of thirst,
I always knew it was you who came first,
Well maybe you *are* mighty quick on the draw,
But cowboy you're slow with the fodder and straw,
Look at me pardner, I'm all skin and bone,
So tonight I ride into the sunset ... alone.

He'll have a shock when he comes out of there,
Me, with four legs sticking up in the air,
Don't say goodbye or thanks for the ride,
My friend it's too little, too late. I have died.
Won't somebody lift up the old saddle flaps,
And gently unbuckle the filthy old straps,
My eyes have grown weary, I'm tired of talk,
And as from tonight, he can bloody well walk.

## Not Cricket

I detested cricket when I wrote this. It seemed endless, I couldn't understand the rules, and it always seemed to take place in the most uncomfortable and spiflicating heat.

Another thing that coloured my view was that my husband (who loves the game) and I once accepted an invitation to a cricket weekend in Scarborough. This was organised by one of the big supermarkets and sounded enticing because the journey to Scarborough was on a train drawn by the celebrated Mallard steam locomotive. That part was interesting and memorable, but the weekend that followed didn't do much for me. As usual, I was bored stiff by the cricket and depressed by the 'freebie' nature of the event, with people falling over themselves to get at the free beer. You can see that my presence added greatly to the cheeriness of the occasion.

However, as time went on and my husband and I had our two sons, I began to see cricket from a different perspective. The boys joined the local village team, and though I still had trouble understanding the rules of the game, I could see a lot of pleasant things taking place. The team were nice blokes, who welcomed our sons and their cricketing friends. When I went along to watch, I fell into friendly conversation with the associated wives, girlfriends, children and dogs. I drank cups of tea and helped to finish up the cakes on lovely, sunny summer days, and when I wielded a tea cloth and dried up the crocks I felt a kindly connection to the generations of women who had stood on that bit of the threadbare pavilion carpet before me. I saw that a little hard-up cricket club like ours could be an intensely benign place, where camaraderie, friendship, support and general mickey-taking enhance people's lives.

So I have kindly feelings towards cricket now. I no longer even try to understand the rules, but definitely count myself a fan.

## *Not Cricket*

The sun is beating down and we are seated at the ground,
You alert beside me drinking in the sight and sound,
Your every nerve is straining, rapt attention is assured,
So what cannot be machine-gunned will just have to be endured.

The gilded first eleven is upon the hallowed pitch,
One is us and one is them, don't ask me which is which,
Languidly the captains gather round to toss a coin,
And someone rubs a ball with relish up and down his groin.

What mouldering eternity the hours take to pass,
I gaze up at the sky and then I gaze down at the grass,
Innings come and go, they hit a six, they hit a four,
We might be in the lead but then again I can't be sure.

I see you there beside me, not a flicker, not a twitch,
You are mesmerised and I am bored to fever pitch,
The ball goes rolling by with someone hard upon its heels,
A player has been stumped and I know just the way he feels.

A gentleman in front of me has taken this quite hard,
He mops his brow and testily he scribbles on his card,
In his thinning hair I see a wasp become ensnared,
It stung him when the score was fifty-one for two declared.

The endless walking on the field, the endless walking back,
The mute incomprehension as the scoreboard starts to clack,
The talk is of the overs and the Series and the Test,
While out of the pavilion come beery shouts of jest.

Those tired cricket stories, how they never fail to bore,
That bowling maidens over joke, I've heard it all before,
Silly mid-ons, googlies, how they all begin to pall,
And so too does that story where the umpire shouts 'No Ball!'

But wait! There's been a ripple and I think someone is hit,
Yes! The ball has struck the batsman and he's staggering a bit,
He's reeling to the left-hand side and reeling to the right,
This is the most gripping moment since we came on Monday night

The physio is racing to the knot of stricken men,
He opens up his case and there's Emergency Ward 10,
But the batsman's on his feet. Oh no, it's all gone very dull,
I thought he had concussion or perhaps a fractured skull.

BORED? I must be the most BORED spectator left alive,
Can't tell if I've been sitting here for three days or for five,

If it was bull-fighting and the matador was gored,
There might be something to laugh at but quite candidly I'm BORED

A social outcast, cricket is no music to my ears,
I've been here for a century and I am bored to tears,
The day is over! God at last has hearkened to my prayer,
And I think we won the ashes. I don't know … and I DON'T CARE!

## I Am Going to Kill My Husband

I am going to kill my husband,
I have stuck all I can stick,
His constant criticising
Is getting on my wick,
He takes it all for granted,
But tonight I can relax,
For the minute he complains,
I shall whop him with the axe.

Yes, I'm going to kill my husband,
I shall have him to be sure,
He's never going to curse
My navigation any more,
I drive him to distraction
When I read a map, I know,
But tonight I'm going to drive him
Where he didn't plan to go.

So when he starts haranguing me
Till I'm a nervous wreck,
Shouts and spits and rages

Till the veins swell in his neck,
As he grabs the map from me
There'll be no turning back,
I will calmly reach behind me
And I'll whop him with the jack.

I mean. He gets a cold
And I'm supposed to sympathise,
And his sneezes shake the rafters
And the tears roll from his eyes,
He looks so woebegone,
Just like the back end of a bus,
And yet when *I* am ill
He'll tell *me* not to make a fuss.

It's true, he's got to go,
You may not not think I've got the right,
But he snores you see and I should know
I'm with him every night,
With a horrifying steady rythmn
Whistle, snore and snort,
Well tonight he's going to stay asleep
For longer than he thought.

Your Honour I confess,
That with a satisfying thwack,
I hit him with the frying pan
From seven paces back,
The weapon was examined
By the jury good and true,
It was all made up of women,
And they all said ... 'After you!'

## The Pregnancy Poem

I had my first child at 35 and my second at 37, so I've always felt very fortunate to have two cracking sons despite leaving it so late.

I liked being pregnant. I found it fascinating, if a little disturbing, the way that my body suddenly ignored me like some old cast-off and got busy with the baby. I took my place on an assembly line of ante-natal classes, visits to the doctor and mysterious government forms that I never knew existed. I pored over catalogues offering maternity wear, trousers with vast elasticated panels at the front and gargantuan bras with trapdoors. I stood ready with bulging tubes of unguent to strike back at stretch marks as soon as they appeared. Pregnancy was a different world, temporarily inhabited and absorbing. I wrote this account of it when I was, as my mother would have put it, eight months gone.

### *The Pregnancy Poem*

Dear Mum, I have achieved the state
Of pregnancy at last,
I know you thought that I
Had let my chances fritter past
I know you had despaired
Of seeing any child of mine
But Mother! I have cracked it
At the age of ninety-nine!

I'm diligently going to
The ante-natal classes
They've issued me a card

To get me free false teeth and glasses
They've got a practice baby
You can bath and put to bed
It's only made of rubber
You can drop it on its head.

I'm taking vitamins
In case my diet is in doubt
I'm taking Brewers Yeast
To stop my hair from falling out
I'm drinking pints of milk
Because the calcium they say
Will give him mighty fangs
As he goes gnashing on his way.

I'm eating meat and fish and eggs
And bread with wholemeal flour
And every afternoon
I put me feet up for an hour
I practise relaxation
To reduce the labour pains
And wear elastic stockings
To unvaricose me veins.

I've bought a fancy pram
In which to push him round the place
I'm rigging up a net
To keep the cat from off his face
I've bought a safety harness
So he cannot up and flee
When he's looking for his mother
And he notices it's me.

You asked me how I am, Mum
And I mustn't carry on
I'm not sick every morning
And the rash is nearly gone
I get a bit of backache
And me ankles tend to swell
But apart from heartburn, cramp
And sleepless nights, I'm very well.

Well Mum, that's all for now
Because I've got so much to do
And every twenty minutes
I am rushing to the … garden
I thought I'd write a letter
Just to tell you how I am
From me, your everloving daughter
Pregnant Poet Pam.

## Wayne

Our eldest son was born in December 1982 in the John Radcliffe Hospital, Oxford. It was a long and tiring business but was, at the same time, the most vivid and miraculous experience I had ever had – until the next little boy came along, when the whole process was re-enacted but a lot faster.

After the first birth I felt absolutely finished, and the baby was put into the nursery so that I could have an undisturbed sleep. When I woke up I hurried out to the nursery to fetch him. A baby had been stolen from another hospital at about that time, and security in all maternity wards had been stepped up. I had to wait outside the nursery and look at the babies in their cots through thick glass. When they let me in I shot over to my own son. There were a dozen babies there, and none of them meant anything to me except mine, who meant everything. It sounds obvious, I know, but then it was a new and marvellous feeling for me, that homing in on your own child – his smell, the shape of his head, the little, scraggy neck. Clearly, nobody else's baby was a patch on mine ...

## Wayne

My baby's eyes are bluer than yours
He's got much more hair and he's stronger
He's ever so bright
He sleeps through the night
And of our two I'd say mine is longer
I swear it's the truth
Mine's cutting a tooth
And he's obviously going to be tall
No, it's hard to explain
Now I've looked at your Wayne
Why *you* bothered to have one at all.

## *Poor Dad*

My wife was a lovely girl
A friend right from the start
We had good times together
Never cared to be apart
We went on lovely holidays
But now all that's gone west
For my wife's had a baby
And I am second best.

She won't come to the pictures
And she won't come for a drink
She's making eggy bread
Or washing bottles in the sink
She will not take my hand
Although I am the man she loves
No, she's nappy sterilising
In a set of rubber gloves.

Either she is feeding him
Or tickling his tum
Patting him or stroking him
Or trying to suck his thumb
Then there's great excitement
When she holds him on the pot
I think if he performed
She'd have convulsions on the spot.

And when at last she's laid him
Tenderly into his cot
There he lies surrounded
By the trappings he has got
And leaning over all
I see the back view of his mother
Cranking up a mobile
Playing something or the other.

And hanging in his cot
He has a finger practice thing
And if he pokes or prods it
It will whirr and clonk and ding
At half past four each morning
Not a morning has he missed
He whirrs and clonks and dings
And drives his father round the twist.

And all across the carpet
Where I used to stretch me legs
Are his rattles, and his beakers
And his half-chewed Bickiepegs
His pram, his little buggy
With the sunshade for his head
No don't tidy up
I'll go and sit out in the shed

Last night for example
I had just come in from work
I'm glad no one was watching
Or I should have felt a berk
I burst in through the door
And I was throttled as I came
By the cables of a baby bouncer
Hanging from the frame.

He *is* a lovely baby
Anyone can plainly see
But while I'm fond of him
He hasn't got much time for me
Frankly as a dad
I feel a failure and a dunce
When I appear he cries
And sicks and widdles all at once.

She's locked the bathroom cabinet
She's making such a fuss
I have to pick the padlock
Just to get me shaving brush
His little pots and bottles

Are clustered round the tap
For soothing gums and iffy tums
And nasty cradle cap.

I mustn't wake the baby up
Or give the door a slam
I mustn't mow the lawn
Because he's out there in his pram
I mustn't play my records
She's got noises on the brain
It's 'Must you blow your nose?'
And 'Did you *have* to pull the chain?'

Ah well, I've had me sandwich
So I'll clear off down the pub
I doubt my wife will notice
For they've both got in the tub
There's laughing and there's splashing
A good time's being had
'Well bye bye dear!'
Oh. She can't hear.
'Try not to miss me ... Dad.'

## *Mirror Song*

Who's that boy in the mirror?
Who can that little boy be?
He's always there when I'm there
And he looks a lot like me
Oh
When I wear my blue trousers
He wears his too
And that little boy's mummy
She looks a lot like you.

## *Where Did You Get ... ?*

Where did you get a little round tum like that from?
Where did you get a little round tum like that from?
Mum's and Dad's are not like that
Mum's and Dad's are nice and flat
So where did you get a little round tum
A little round tum like yours?

and

Where did you get two little teeth like that from?
Where did you get two little teeth like that from?
Not one bit like Mummy or Dad
Mum's and Dad's teeth all went bad
So where did you get two little teeth
Two little teeth like yours?

and

Where did you get a sticky little face like that from?
Where did you get a sticky little face like that from?
The stickiest face I've ever seen
Mummy's and Dad's are nice and clean
So where did you get a sticky little face
A sticky little face like yours?

## Whose Toes Are Those?

Whose toes are those?
Mine I suppose
*And* fingers, what luck!
I'll give them a suck.

## New Baby

Dear Mum, A little letter while the baby is asleep
I've tucked him in his cot and put the nappies in to steep
I took the bottle teat because his feeding seemed so slow
And stabbed it with a safety pin to quicken up the flow.

I haven't learned the knack of how to bath the baby yet
He seems to get so angry that he baths himself with sweat
And when I get him in it after dithering about
He widdles in the water and I have to take him out.

But if the days are difficult, the nights are harder still
I'm not one to complain but well perhaps today I will
I'm sleeping in my cosy bed and everything's all right
When a little hungry whimpering comes stealing through the night.

And off into the gloom we go, the baby and the mother
Slowly down the landing holding on to one another
I know he's only little and I know he must be fed
But I'd give a thousand pounds if I could jump back into bed.

You see I haven't had a decent sleep for weeks and weeks
But still I gamely dab the bottled roses on me cheeks
My lovely shiny hair that used to bounce about before
Is clogging up the hairbrush in the dressing table drawer.

I'm so tired Mother and my muscles seem so slack
They say that doing exercise will bring my figure back
My lovely tummy, flatter than the surface of a lake
Feels just like a plate of that blancmange you used to make.

So in the afternoon I have a nap, a little rest
An easy thing to do, a normal person would suggest
I curl up on the sofa with the papers on the floor
And half a dozen people start to hammer on the door.

Friends I haven't seen for years are there in overcoats
In they troop with coughs and colds and ulcerated throats

211

I have to give them cups of tea, I have to give them cake
And underneath my breath I think 'Push off for goodness sake!'

I'll cook the dinner now and peg the nappies on the line
Mum, I'll have to go but yes the babe and me are fine
I'd walk him in his pram but now it's gone in for repairs
I'm afraid it got a rupture when I heaved it down the stairs.

Love to everyone at home and will you tell them all
Thank you for the knitted coats. Every one's too small.
I'll have to love and leave you, there is wailing from on high
Did I make the right decision, Mother? Yes! Goodbye.

## Baby's Dinner Time

It's time to have my dinner
Half past twelve has come
My shouting and complaining
Have proved too much for Mum
It might be Bovril soldiers
Or egg and bacon tart
It might be mashed banana
But it's time to make a start.

Mum puts me in my high chair
And stands it by the wall
She gets the bib and harness
And the suction plate and all
I push my feet against the table
Not too low or high

So the chair goes over backwards
And I bump my head and cry.

And then I get impatient
And rattle on my plate
And struggle in my high chair
So that Mum gets in a state
I take my teacher beaker
And whirl it by the spout
With any luck the lid comes off
And all the drink flies out.

Mum's keen on table manners
If a visitor has come
It's always 'Sit up nicely now'
and 'Eat it up for Mum'
So what I like to do
Is take a mouthful of the food
And smiling at the guest
I let it tumble out half-chewed.

Some I suck and swallow
Some I suck and leave
Some sticks in me hair
And quite a lot sticks on me sleeve
Mum gets irritated
When I give the bowl a stir
So before she takes my spoon away
I stick a bit on her.

Mummy's had no dinner
She isn't looking bright

She's looking very tired
Still I grizzled half the night
Her eyelids keep on closing
Her chin is on her chest
Of all the things we do each day
My mum likes dinner time best.

## Nanny

The day our nanny got the sack
The baby slipped up round the back
Bumped his head and grazed his knee
And ran to her and not to me.

## Foghorn Lullaby

Go to sleep my little foghorn
Give your poor old throat a rest
Of all the little foghorns
You're the one I love the best
You're the dearest little foghorn
In the country or the town
But how I sometimes wish
That I could turn the volume down!

## Do You Think Bruce Springsteen
## Would Fancy Me?

I had the idea for this one Christmas Eve when our children were small. Anxious to look as though I were coping admirably, I unwisely invited a great gang of people for Christmas lunch. I should never have done this because, much as I esteemed them all, I was exhausted and not up to it. Two little boys late in life and close together had just about done for me. The massive lunch loomed regardless.

On Christmas Eve it was midnight before our boys were in bed and asleep, and all the top-secret business had been finished. I was desperate to go to bed myself, but there was no hope of that. Instead I had to start preparing the gargantuan meal with which I had saddled myself. I looked sourly at the strewn kitchen. A vast white turkey lay legs akimbo, showing its enormous, as yet unstuffed cavity. Mountains of sprouts waited to be trimmed and have a little cross cut into their stalks, then bread sauce, chipolatas rolled in bacon, roast potatoes, chestnuts, pudding and everything else waited in line. I knew all these jobs would take me until dawn, and that then I was supposed to look like the saintly mother and radiant hostess. I could have cried.

Desperate for some distraction, I switched on the TV. It was midnight, and a rock concert was being beamed in live from the States. A voice from the abyss boomed out across the vast stadium: 'Ladies and gentlemen, will you please put your hands together and welcome on to the stage MR BRUCE SPRINGSTEEN!' A roar of excitement and anticipation went up from the audience. I had never heard of him in my life.

Out on to the stage he walked, picked up his guitar, stood in front of his band, the E Street Band, and started to sing 'Born in the USA'. I stopped stuffing the turkey and looked at him with mounting interest. He had brown shiny hair and a red bandanna. The sleeves of his black T-shirt had been ripped off to expose pulsating biceps. He wore motor-bike boots, black jeans and a thick, riveted leather belt such as you might put round the neck of a Rottweiler. Things were looking up.

From feeling utterly dejected and defeated I now felt uplifted and energized. The sight of Bruce and the sound of his thunderous music transformed my mood, and I danced round the kitchen on my own, feeling positive and smoulderingly attractive. Unfortunately, my dancing feet took me past the oven, mounted half-way up the kitchen wall. In it I could see my reflection.

It was a sobering sight. I felt as if a balloon had been pricked. The way I felt did not correspond with the way I looked. All round

my eyes I could see the tiny lines, and the grey bits of my hair showing where I had not slapped the preparation on it. I remembered that I had a gammy knee: it's not gammy all the time, but if my trousers get wet it throbs for a week. Round my neck I could see the glasses for close work, and the work seems to be getting closer all the time. I thought to myself, 'You look so stupid, jigging round the kitchen thinking salacious thoughts about Bruce Springsteen. You're too old – it's time to start acting with dignity and restraint, as befits a woman of a certain age.' This is the resultant ballad, a kind of lament for my lost gorgeousness.

### Do You Think Bruce Springsteen Would Fancy Me?

Do you think Bruce Springsteen would fancy me?
I know I've just turned forty-three,
And one eye's gone at a funny angle,
And I have to wear a copper bangle,
As I've got arthritis in this left knee,
But d'you think Bruce Springsteen would fancy me?

He might like an older bird,
Someone not of the common herd,
Old and inhibition free,
Well he need look no further than me,
I've lost the looks that once I had,
But then perhaps his eyesight's bad,
My skin's quite good, and me teeth – fantastic!
Crafted from the finest plastic,
So next weekend at the NEC,
Do you think Bruce Springsteen would fancy me?

He might like to dance with me,
If I keep the weight off me gammy knee,
But there again, me kneecaps click,
Still, I needn't take me walking stick.
No, I'd be like a magnet to him,
The sight of me would go straight through him,
One boss eye and me hair gone grey,
Singing 'Born in the USA'.

Course, Bruce is used to admiration,
He's idolised in every nation,
Cheered and clapped in every state,
Me? I'm clapped at half past eight.
Me husband says I must be mad,
And didn't I know Bruce Springsteen had
Teenage bimbos wall to wall,
Young and slim and brown and tall,
They can dance and stay up late,
Their knees don't click and their eyes go straight,
He says Bruce wants rock and rhythm,
Not some old bird's rheumatism.

But I don't care, I know I'm right,
At the NEC next Friday night,
Though there might be thousands there,
Our eyes will meet in a thrilling stare,
I'll do me slow seductive grin,
I hope to God me teeth stay in,
And in that flash of recognition,
Bruce and I will have ... ignition.

Draw the veil on he and I,
Alone against the starlit sky,
The billows pound upon the shore,
And me clicking knee will be heard ... no more.

## Don't Start!

I was on a ferry boat one dark night, sailing from Heysham near Liverpool to Douglas in the Isle of Man. I was going to do a performance in the Gaiety Theatre. It was a very rough night, the decks were wet, and the sea looked black and terrifying. That particular ferry boat had an extra refinement, a Ladies' Lounge, so if you didn't want to contaminate yourself by sitting next to a man, you could go and sit in there. I was lonely and unnerved by the conditions, so I did.

There was only one other person there, a young woman prostrate with seasickness, lying limp and exhausted on one of the couches. Her poor face had turned a dismal green-grey, she gripped a paper bag and lay enduring the hours of misery.

Her problem was made worse by the fact that she was accompanied by her small son, a bright, lively little boy of about three. From time to time he would come up to his mother and give her a good shake. 'Mum!' he would shout, 'MUM!', and in a voice of abject misery she would reply, 'Oh, don't start ...'

To my eternal shame, I did nothing, but looked on like a great buffoon. This was not so much because I didn't want to help – it was just that I didn't know what to do. Until I had my own children, I was clueless; I had very little in the way of maternal instincts at all. Years later, when I found I was expecting a child myself, I went to talk to my mother about my lack of maternal feeling. She was very reassuring and said, 'Don't you worry about that, because the love comes with it.' It did, but I still think it's cutting it a bit fine.

Anyway, back on the boat I did not help this poor woman, and we sailed on gloomily, the hours punctuated by her saying, 'Oh, don't start, don't start.' The phrase stayed in my mind. Years later I often uttered it warningly to my own family, and I bet if you listen to any exasperated mum in the supermarket today you wouldn't have to wait long to hear it again.

The little scene on the ferry is where this idea came from, and in this poem I have gone to visit my mum, taking with me my little son Richard, aged three ...

## *Don't Start!*

Hello Mum! We're here!
What awful traffic round the place!
Richard! In you come,
Don't push the door in Grandma's face!
Making sure we brought it all,
That's been the hardest part,
*RICHARD*! Don't do that!
Get down! Come here! Sit still! Don't start!

We had to come this morning,
It's the only chance we've got,
Dad'll need the car this week,
He's travelling a lot,
He sold the van, he advertised it
In *Exchange and Mart*,
*RICHARD!* Put that back! Don't touch!
Now then! D'you hear? Don't start!

How's your ear? No better?
Have it syringed, Mum, go today,
I had mine syringed in April,
I fell over all that day,
We didn't have the dog put down,
We didn't have the heart,
*DON'T YOU PUT THAT IN YOUR MOUTH!*
I'm warning you! Don't start!

You said you'd be a good boy,
But I haven't seen it yet,
Now look what Granny's given you,
A little ... dartboard set,
Don't just throw the paper down!
*NO! DON'T YOU THROW THAT DART!*
*WHAT* a good thing Granny ducked!
Behave yourself. Don't start.

I've done the tea,
Well by this afternoon I'll start to flag,
I made us Gourmet Beef,
You had to boil it in the bag,
Dad likes a home-made pudding,
So I bought a Bakewell Tart,
No! You *can't* have some now!
Sit up! Don't answer back! Don't start!

What? Is that the time?
Half past eleven! What a shock,
Back we go then,
Dad'll want the car for two o'clock,
Look at all this junk!
We should have brought a horse and cart,
*LOOK OUT!* How many more times?
Now look what you've done! Don't start!

Say 'Bye Bye' to Granny
And say 'Thanks for having me'
Richard! Kiss your gran,
Now, come on! Switch off that TV!
*SHE HAS NOT GOT WHISKERS*, Richard!
Don't you be so smart!
You thank her for a lovely time,
That's it. Bye Mum … and don't start.

## *The Ballad of the Bungleclud*

In the marshes, thick with mud
Lies the dreadful Bungleclud
In the bog up to his eyes
There he watches, there he spies
Still, except for fingers drumming
Looking out for people coming.

Bunglecluds are large and hairy
And their eyes are quick and wary
Watching out for signs of joggers
Ice-cream men or stray hot-doggers
English teachers, you or me
Or anyone to have for tea.

Bunglecluds are dark and wrinkled
And their tails are long and crinkled
On their ears are tufts of hair
That twitch and flicker everywhere
And both their nostrils red and flared
Are good for making people scared.

But oh, his mouth so wide and black
With great big tonsils down the back
And jagged teeth from left to right
No fillings, caps or crowns in sight
And Bunglebreath so foul and smelly
Turns most people's knees to jelly.

Lying in the mud so long
Causes Bunglecluds to pong
When it gets too much to bear
Up they get and out they tear
Climbing madly up the trees
To have an airing in the breeze.

When Bunglecluds no longer hum
Down to earth refreshed, they come
They promenade along the grass
And to Bunglecluds they pass
Enquire 'How is your sainted mother?'
And sweetly smile at one another.

Bunglecluds are rarely seen
But anywhere that mud is green
And deep and dark and nasty smelling
Go with caution! There's no telling!
Bubbles rising from the deep
Could mean a Bungleclud ... Asleep!

## Cling to me Nigel

Cling to me Nigel, Oh cling to me do,
There's only one man that I love and it's you,
You're handsome and charming, exactly my sort,
My only regret is you're two feet too short.

I know it's a thing that nobody can help,
But I get so tired of addressing your scalp,
They say good things come in small parcels it's true,
But I've never seen parcels come smaller than you.

Oh cling to me Nigel, we'll kick up our heels,
We'll dance round the floor to the jigs and the reels,
Although other people may snigger and laugh,
For you my beloved, are too short by half.

When I am with you my joy is complete,
I'd just like to stretch you a couple of feet,
And when we are dancing and whirling around,
Oh why is it *your* feet that come off the ground?

When he whispers sweet nothings, I miss what he said,
Because I gaze down at the top of his head,
But cling to me Nigel, you have me beguiled,
Your ear on my bosom is driving me wild.

I bought him a ladder, I bought him a box,
I bought fertiliser to stick in his socks,
But cling to me Nigel, although you're not tall,
A little one is better than no one at all.

## Who's Had My Scissors?

WHO'S HAD MY SCISSORS? It just isn't *fair*
I left them right here on the arm of my chair,
I know that you all live in chaos, that's fine,
But this little corner, this cupboard, it's MINE!

I know you think 'Oh Mum's just having a moan,'
But the *times* that I've bought you a pair of your own,
I bought little red ones with safe rounded ends,
To try and prevent you from stabbing your friends.

I've bought pencil cases with scissors in too
But where are they now? Oh, we haven't a clue!

## The Works

I know you're too busy to listen to me,
Slumped on the sofa all watching TV.

I know. I shall find them in some muddy crater
Out in the garden a week or two later
There they will be at the end of the hunt,
Rusty and buckled and horribly blunt.

It's just that I'd hoped for a moment or two,
To pick up my stitching and finish the blue,
To whip up the side in a flurry of tacks,
And cut off the thread with a ruddy great axe.

My scissors are missing. You may not have heard.
They're silver and wrought in the shape of a bird,
In a pouch of red leather with fol de rols on
And while I don't wish to sound boring … they've GONE!

Wait! Someone is answering, this is a treat!
Of *course* I have looked down the side of my seat
What? *So they are!* Down the side of the chair!
All right. Tell the truth. Which of you put them there?

## The Voice at the Foot of the Stairs

When our sons were small, I was always exhausted by the hour spent getting them up and getting them off to school. I would arise in the morning feeling reasonably serene and on top of things, but by the time I had finally got them out of the door I was at a standstill, at my wits' end. It seemed that we went through the same scenarios each morning; nobody learnt anything from the last time – the same old, familiar crises loomed day after day. We fell out so regularly about exactly the same things that I began to keep a notebook at the bottom of the stairs, where I scrawled the usual flashpoints as they flashed. My hope in doing this was that when times were calmer, I could write something based on them that would strike a familiar chord with other parents.

## The Voice at the Foot of the Stairs

It's twenty-five past seven boys,
I've boiled you both an egg,
Up you get then! Rise and shine!
Let's have you! Shake a leg!
Twenty-five past seven!
Breakfast's ready! Don't all flock!
(I used to be important,
Now I'm just the speaking clock.)

It's five to eight! It's five to eight,
You've cut it very fine!
I see you've combed your hair,
It's stuck up like a porcupine
Have you washed your hands?
That looks suspiciously like dirt,
Pass the milk, look out, too late!
It's gone all down his shirt.

Let go of the cereal!
You'll have it on the floor!
Does it *really* matter
That he had the toy before?
Here's your football boot!
It's where you left it Friday night,
It's got no studs or laces,
But the rest of it's all right.

Have you fed the rabbit?
The goldfish does look queer.
You gave him *too* much breakfast!
Still, I s'pose the tank will clear,
Hurry up then boys,
Because it's nearly time to leave,
D'you want a handkerchief?
Or can you manage with your sleeve?

Does anybody want to go
Who's not already been?
Then brush your face and wash your teeth,
It's nearly eight-fifteen.
Why can't you lace your trainer?
Try not to lose control,
You've lost the pointed bit
That's meant to push it through the hole.

Now put your shoes on properly,
And *don't stand on the backs!*
HE DOESN'T WANT A RUGBY TACKLE!
Calm down and relax,
He's looking for his *other* shoe,
his homework and his coat,
And he'll find them quicker still
without you clinging to his throat.

Oh. You're finishing your homework.
I don't believe it's true,
You should have done it yesterday!
It's twenty minutes to!

Who was in the basket?
How am I supposed to know?
Moses? John the Baptist?
Or the bullrush? I dunno.

Come on! Here's the bus!
It's ten to nine, right on the dot,
Off you go, bye bye,
See you tonight, don't pick your spot.
Do stop aggravating him!
I saw you throw that punch!
Bye! Mind how you go!
    And by the way ...
        You've left your lunch ...

## A Little Visitor

Ugh! I don't like meat, and I can't eat cheese,
I like *Mum's* cakes but I couldn't fancy these,
It's boring here, do I *have* to stay?
And I wish I hadn't bothered coming *here* to play.

Can I have a Fanta? Can I have a Coke?
Is that *your* dad? He's a dodgy looking bloke,
Can I watch telly? *Home and Away*?
They were fighting with a crocodile yesterday.

Can I have a bag of crisps? Can I have two?
UGH! Not *plain*, are there any barbecue?

## Pam Ayres

Your dog's scratched me! Look he's left a place!
*That* is why I had to go and kick him in the face.

Have you got a Game Boy? Can I have a go?
Can I have a borrow of your Nintendo?
Any new computer games? Not as good as *me*
*I've* got an Atari and a BBC.

I'm absolutely starving, are we *ever* having tea?
When *my* mum cooks the sausages they have to wait for *me*,
They're *always* on the table and there's *never* a delay,
And I *never* have to tidy up, I just go out to play.

I never hittim! That's not true!
I never laid a finger on him! Bleghh* to you
I never did it, I wasn't there,
And even if I hadda been, I don't care!

I tried your bike, oh, I left it in the rain,
I rode it up the cobbles, something happened to the chain,
You should have heard the racket when I rode it down
    the stairs,
There's a good shop in the High Street if it wants a few
    repairs.

*\*He makes a horrible face at this point!*

## A–Z

Driving in London's my pleasure
I prize it above any other.
One hand on the wheel,
The fingers like steel,
And the A–Z clenched
In the other.

## *The Policeman*

Dear Dad, You've always told me the policeman guards the weak,
And if ever I'm in trouble he's the person I should seek,
You've told me how he labours night and day with little thanks,
Catching thugs and criminals and people robbing banks,
How he does his best to keep us safe and keep us sound,
And how all decent people are relieved when he's around.
And yet Dad, when we drove to Auntie Jean's the other day,
And that policeman made you stop along the motorway,
When he pressed that little piece of paper in your hand,
Well, you made all those suggestions that I did not understand.
Long after he had gone you kept on clawing back your hair,
And making all those strange two-fingered gestures in the air,
You ranted and you raved, we had to get out of the car,
And Mother had to fan you with a copy of *The Star*.
What worries me if he's our friend, and that *is* what you said,
Is what you'd do if he'd have been an enemy instead.

## Jones, the Invisible Man of the Third

I wrote this because I was asked to open a new art department at a college and was expected to make a short speech. I love drawing and painting, but I couldn't just say that. What I really wanted to say was that I believe everybody is good at something. It may be that your particular something is quite different from all the rest, but a good school should seek it out terrier-like, do its very best to discover and develop every pupil's special strength.

Here, the talent of poor little hapless Jones, previously so invisible, is spotted. He has a painting chosen for the Art Exhibition, and this achievement is all it takes to pluck him from the anonymous throng. Suddenly he is a somebody, as he receives the most priceless of simple gifts: the pat on the back.

## *Jones, the Invisible Man of the Third*

Jones of the Third was not sporty at all,
He was poorly adapted for kicking a ball,
No study of maths irresistibly drew him
And transitive verbs were a mystery to him,
The French mistress did not succumb to his charm
In Woodwork he planed all the skin off his arm
Girls didn't like him or think he was nice,
Didn't look once, never mind about twice.

The choir didn't want him, he knew that for sure,
He'd warbled a psalm but they'd shown him the door
So while those around him to glory were spurred
He remained the invisible man of the Third.
In Pottery, Jones thought his moment had come
Such a pot did he make that the tutor was dumb
It was huge, all artistically gilded and caked
But alas it exploded while still being baked.

One morning however when light in the heart
He arrived feeling kindly disposed towards Art
He painted a picture, and thought it was good,
Of a field and a tree and a cow and a wood.
The Art Master came, picked it up, put it down
Saying 'Excellent work, I commend you young … Brown.'
And Jones found himself in the heady position
Of having work sent for the Art Exhibition.

And when the day came and he went to the hall
And saw his framed picture up there on the wall
Well, he stopped being Jones of no obvious charm
Jones, who had planed all the skin off his arm,
Jones, never noble heroic or brave
Giving no indication of needing to shave
Jones who the girls never looked at at all,
or Jones who was useless at kicking a ball. ...

He was Jones, of the Third, recognised and acclaimed
Mentioned wherever True Artists were named,
Who greeted the Head with a nonchalant wave
Who any day now would be needing to shave,
Who, handsome and charming would sweep through
    the town
Brushing the girls from the hem of his gown
The *first* in a long and time honoured tradition
Of having work shown – in the Art Exhibition.

## The Unisex Salon

O hand me down the aspirin, the warm sustaining tea,
Hold my feeble shaking hand and try to comfort me,
I went to have my hair done, I shall never go again,
They've made the salon unisex. They've started doing MEN!

A MAN was at the basin, leaning confidently back,
Though I hope like me it made his neck feel fit to crack,
I had to step across him, I can see his trainers yet,
And seeing him, I felt myself bedraggled plain and wet.

What's he doing here with us, breathing healthy spray,
Watching the assistants as they give the game away,
We come to be coloured, streaked and tenderly blow-dried,
And permed and titivated and WE WANT THAT MAN OUTSIDE!

Men should be in a barber's shop in a great big barber's chair,
Where a great big barber plies his trade in a great big pile of hair,
Where the carburettor's King, the wicket and the goal,
And men are in their rightful place beneath the barber's pole.

## I'm the Dog Who Didn't Win a Prize

I was invited to a fund-raising day at a large dogs' home in Evesham, Worcestershire. There were various stalls, and the highlight of the day was a light-hearted dog show featuring classes like Dog with the Waggiest Tail, Dog the Judge Would Most Like to Take Home, Best Taker of the Tit-bit, that sort of thing. My job was to walk round with their good-looking vet and help with the judging. When it came to the Most Beautiful Bitch class, I gave the prize to a little dog with a sweet face and exceptionally dark, appealing eyes. Afterwards the vet told me that she had some eye disorder, one symptom of which is that the eyes appear particularly large and moist. This was a bit unfortunate, but overall it was a pleasant, sunny day, raising money for a good cause.

As the event wound up, people and their dogs began to drift away, and many of the dogs wore rosettes and ribbons so they could show off once they got home. One small, disgruntled-looking dog passed, and he seemed to look back over his shoulder at me in an indignant and miffed fashion. He was a little, dark, long-haired dog of the dachshund type, with large, tufted ears. And no rosette.

## *I'm the Dog Who Didn't Win a Prize*

I'm the dog who didn't win a prize.
I didn't have the Most Appealing Eyes.
All day in this heat, I've been standing on me feet
With dogs of every other shape and size.

I've been harshly disinfected, I've been scrubbed,
I've been festooned in a towel and I've been rubbed;
I've been mercilessly brushed, robbed of all me fleas and dust
And now the judging's over: I've been snubbed!

Was it for obedience I was hailed?
As 'Best Dog in the Show' was I regaled?
O not on your Doggo life, pass me down the carving knife,
I had one thing said about me – it was 'FAILED'.

I never for a moment thought I'd fail.
I thought at least I'd win 'Waggiest Tail'.
But no certificate, rosette or commendation did I get –
Nothing on a kennel door to nail.

I am going in my kennel on my own.
Thank you, no. I do not want a bone.
Do not think you can console me with left-overs in my bowl
Me pride is mortified – I want to be alone.

I've heard it from the worldly and the wise:
'Each dog has his day' they all advise,
But I see to my grief and sorrow, my day must have been
    tomorrow!
Oh I'm the dog who didn't win a prize!


## John Joe Polonio

John Joe Polonio, he loved to wear a hat,
He had a balaclava, he was ever so fond of that,
He had a boater made of straw for wearing on a punt,
And he also had a turban with a diamond on the front.

He had a hat like Turpin when he cried 'Stand and deliver!'
Another one like Nelson which would make your timbers
    shiver,
A topper for that smart occasion made him look a toff,
And a bowler for the office, he could wear it on or off.

He had a jolly sailor's hat for swabbing of the deck,
A Foreign Legion hat to keep the sunshine off his neck,
A bathing cap for when he was considering a swim,
And a stove-pipe hat like Lincoln, (but it wasn't really him.)

He loved to wear a Stetson hat straight from the USA,
And a battered old hill-billy hat for raking up the hay,
In leather hat and goggles he was Biggles in his kite,
While in a sheet with eye-holes he could give his mum a fright.

He wore a tam-o-shanter resting lightly on his scalp,
A hat from Switzerland in which to yodel on an Alp,
A brightly coloured jockey's cap for riding home the winner,
And a chef's hat, stiffly starched, for when he had to cook the
    dinner.

When John Joe got married, his poor bride was in despair,
He could not make up his mind which hat he ought to wear,
This one, that one, small one, flat one, long or short or tall,
He just did not know, so in the end ... he wore them all!

# Index of Titles

# H

# I

# J

**L**

**M**

**N**

**O**

# Index of First Lines

**I**

PAM AYRES has been a regular on television and radio since winning the TV talent show *Opportunity Knocks* in 1975. More than thirty years later, Pam is a regular on BBC Radio 4 in her own series *Ayres on the Air*, as well as on programmes such as *Just a Minute*, *Loose Ends* and *That Reminds Me*. Pam performs her solo stage show throughout Britain and around the world, and she has a huge fan base in the UK, Australia and New Zealand. Her work is also available on CD and DVD, and many of her poems are in school textbooks the world over. Pam is one of Britain's best-loved entertainers and was awarded the MBE in the Queen's Birthday Honours of 2004. For details of Pam's theatre engagements please see www.pamayres.com.